GREEK VASES

Molly and Walter Bareiss Collection

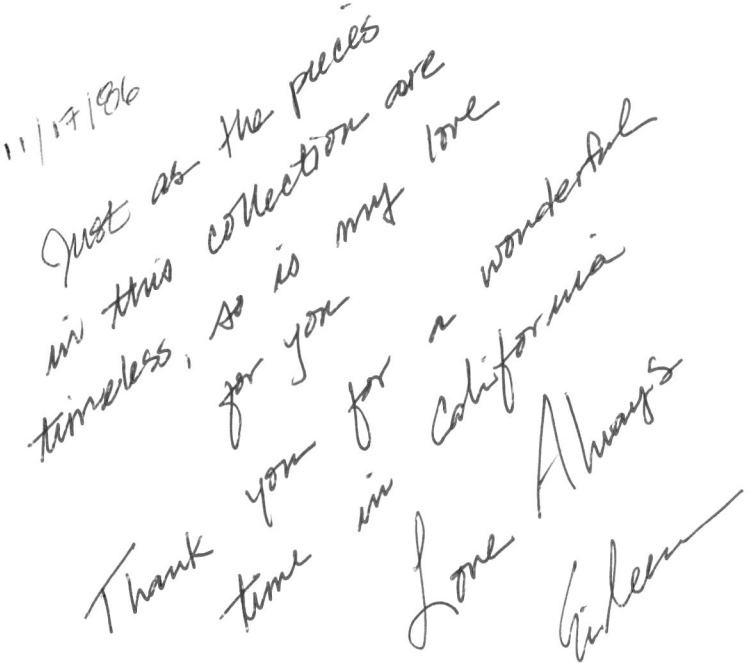

The J. Paul Getty Museum

Malibu, California

Cover: School boy with a lyre facing a bearded man (his instructor?), tondo of a Type B cup signed by the painter Douris; see No. 34, pp. 48–50.

Photography by Penelope Potter, except No. 30 and detail of No. 25 supplied by The Metropolitan Museum of Art, New York.
Design by Patrick Dooley.
Typography by Typographic Service Company, Los Angeles.
Printed by Jeffries Banknote Company, Los Angeles

ISBN no. 0-89236-065-8

"Walter Bareiss as a Collector," by Dietrich von Bothmer (pp. 1–4) is based, by permission, on *The Metropolitan Museum of Art Bulletin*, December 1969, pp. 425–428.

© 1983 The J. Paul Getty Museum
17985 Pacific Coast Highway
Malibu, California
(For information about other Getty Museum publications, please write the Bookstore, The J. Paul Getty Museum, P.O. Box 2112, Santa Monica, California 90406.)

TABLE OF CONTENTS

- iv   PREFACE
- v   ACKNOWLEDGMENTS
- 1   WALTER BAREISS AS A COLLECTOR
- 5   THE WORLD OF GREEK VASES
- 10   FORTY-SEVEN MASTERPIECES FROM THE BAREISS COLLECTION
- 67   CHECKLIST
- 88   GREEK VASE SHAPES

PREFACE

This museum is indeed fortunate to be able to present to the people of Southern California a selection of Greek vases from the remarkable collection of Molly and Walter Bareiss. All of us who enjoy the adventure of history, the search for beauty, and the evidence of scholarship will be grateful for the opportunity to see these 259 examples of some of the finest Attic black-figure and red-figure vases and fragments.

Dietrich von Bothmer has described eloquently in his introduction the significance of the Bareiss Collection, which is undoubtedly the most important collection of its kind still privately owned. In 1969, a smaller selection from this collection was exhibited at the Metropolitan Museum of Art; and another group has been shown at the Yale University Art Gallery. However, not since the dispersal of the Hearst Collection has there been an opportunity for those living on the West Coast to see such a significant group of Greek vases. All who enjoy the perfection of beautiful drawing and significant form must be grateful to Molly and Walter Bareiss for allowing this major selection of Greek vases of the highest quality to be shown at the J. Paul Getty Museum.

OTTO WITTMANN
CHIEF CURATOR

ACKNOWLEDGMENTS

The first contact between Molly and Walter Bareiss and the J. Paul Getty Museum, which has led to this special exhibition, was initiated by the friendly interest of Heinz Herzer.

The understanding of Harold Williams, President of the J. Paul Getty Trust, made the loan of the Bareiss Collection and the preparation of the necessary new exhibition cases possible.

Otto Wittmann, Chief Curator, followed our work with good will and interest. No aspect of the months of preparation for the exhibition could have been accomplished without the constant support of Steven Rountree. The staff of the J. Paul Getty Museum have all contributed to the realization of this exhibition, many above all limits of reasonable expectation. Sally Hibbard, with her usual devotion and the help of John Caswell, settled all the numerous problems connected with the registration of a vast quantity of material. Nearly insurmountable display difficulties were overcome by the team of preparators headed by Bruce Metro. Under the guidance of Zdravko Barov, Patricia Tuttle and Mark A. Kotansky worked — and continue to work — on the conservation of the Bareiss vases. Penelope Potter provided outstanding photographs, only some of which are used in this catalogue. The publication of this illustrated catalogue and checklist and the preparation of other visual materials were achieved in spite of difficult conditions and constant delays thanks to the unselfish devotion of the editor, Sandra Knudsen Morgan, and the museum designer, Patrick Dooley. Various parts of the text were read and improved by Faya Causey Frel, Stanley Moss, and Arthur Houghton.

The realization of the exhibition and of this catalogue and its checklist are due to Marion True and Jiří Frel; the first did more work, the latter feels responsible for any mistakes.

The very existence of the Bareiss Collection owes more than can be said to Dietrich von Bothmer. In 1967, in the last days of Sir John Beazley's activity, he personally introduced Walter Bareiss to 100 Holywell, the home of Sir John, crowning long correspondence between the collector and the Oxford scholar. For years Bothmer himself advised the collector, studied and mended the vases, interpreted the subjects, and traced joins with fragments in other museums, collections, and in the art market. In 1969 he organized a show of the best one hundred vases at the Metropolitan Museum of Art; the checklist of this show was the basis of our work in Malibu. A glance at the checklist at the back of this catalogue will reveal that most of the readings of the inscriptions and the overwhelming majority of the attributions are due to his scholarship. Dietrich von Bothmer, who earned his Ph.D. at Berkeley and became an American citizen in California, understands perhaps better than anyone else the role of Greek and Roman art in the American tradition and hence the importance of making available an outstanding classical collection to the West Coast public. He not only actively assisted in the arrival of the Bareiss vases in Malibu but also did not hesitate to devote his precious time to checking and considerably improving most of the present text to an extent which would justify his full authorship if this would not mean sharing the responsibility for possible errors. The help which he so generously provided to many aspects of the exhibition is only a part of what the classical collection of the J. Paul Getty Museum and the Department of Antiquities owe to him.

The J. Paul Getty Museum and all of us remain obliged to Molly and Walter Bareiss; it is a real pleasure to welcome their collection to Malibu.

WALTER BAREISS AS A COLLECTOR

More than two hundred and fifty vases from the collection of Molly and Walter Bareiss are exhibited in two galleries of the J. Paul Getty Museum, chosen from over five hundred. All of them were collected in the last twenty-five years, and the collection is still growing. When Mr. Bareiss first visited Greece, in 1952, he fell in love with the country and its art. His earliest collecting had centered around Far Eastern art; later he made a name for himself as a collector of modern art; and today his interest is divided between the contemporary and the classical. This does not present a conflict, for Mr. Bareiss is more interested in the personal style of an individual artist than in the general style of a period.

Ever since Mr. Bareiss gave me access to his vases in 1964, I have been fascinated by the constant process of selection and upgrading that is so essential to the formation of a great collection. It is sometimes claimed, and quite wrongly, I think, that wealth alone can bring about almost anything, and that a collection normally represents the income bracket in which a given purchase can be made. This approach tends to ignore something more fundamental: why is money spent at all on works of art? And to what extent can money determine the character of something as personal as a collection of Greek vases? Surely other considerations enter into it. I have known of nobody, even men of almost unlimited wealth, who did not at the moment of purchase have to meet the challenge of a choice—a choice based on preference as much as on cost. No one will claim that it is fashionable to collect Greek vases, and even paying unheard-of prices will not put a collector of Greek vases into newspaper headlines or the annals of auction houses. The very fact that the passion spent on these lesser-known works of art cannot be appreciated by everyone makes such a collector rely more on his own sense of beauty than on popular appeal. Some collectors do not move without counsel; others are as impetuous as a young man in love, and their regrets are less frequently voiced over objects they should not have bought than over masterpieces they lost.

With over fifty thousand Greek painted vases in existence, no single collection can lay claim to being truly representative. The long life of a museum brings with it some measure of assurance that its collection of vases, if worked on steadily, will in time improve; while the supply continues, it is often more a question of budgetary allocation than of opportunities. Here, museums that were able to lay their foundations in the happier days of the nineteenth century and the first years of this, have the advantage of a wealth of examples of recognized quality against which each newcomer is measured. A contemporary collector, on the other hand, must start from scratch. He may envy the ease with which the great private and public collections were formed in the last century, but he may feel compensated in knowing that today's increased knowledge of vase painting helps him to a surer recognition of style than was possible for his predecessors. Appreciation of a painted vase does not, of course, consist solely in dating it or attributing it to a specific artist. Scholarship has advanced in the last sixty years to the point where practically every Greek vase has been or can be attributed, and certain sales catalogues almost exploit scholarly refinements and abound in such catch phrases as "rare," "unique," "unusual," or the like. Remembering the number of vases that exist, a true collector is not easily seduced by such epithets. He must find in the object itself a fulfillment of the desires of his acquisitive instinct.

Mr. Bareiss has been guided by his own ideals of quality and by an all-pervasive sense of curiosity. Some of his vases were bought for the sheer beauty of their shape, but the majority were selected with an eye to the painted decoration. His interest in the subject, coupled with a genuine understanding of quality in drawing, has freed Mr. Bareiss from the quaint prejudice against fragments that is encountered so often. The true connoisseur of painted Greek vases will put greater value on a single figure, incomplete, painted by a master than on a seductively complete vase decorated in haste by a hack. Moreover, his eye will be able to restore an entire figure, or even a whole composition, on sherds that are tantalizingly incomplete. His vases need not be signed; he will recognize artists by the style alone, and he will remember that many of the best vase painters are still anonymous to us and have had to be given distinctive names in modern time.

So far I have spoken of Mr. Bareiss's vases as a whole; the ones on view in the Getty Museum were chosen with several points of view in mind. Apart from the obvious first consideration, artistic quality, an attempt was made not only to show to advantage the entire gamut of the Bareiss Collection but also to supplement the museum's own display. Those who love Greek vases for the sake of their refined shapes will thus detect one of the earliest panel amphorae with flanged handles (No. 5, Checklist no. 25), a kylix exceptional in form and decoration, signed by the potter Nikosthenes (No. 14, Checklist no. 94), and a hydria with rare coloristic touches of white on foot and mouth (No. 9, Checklist no. 60), and will observe the drinking cup from its modest beginning (No. 11, Checklist no. 83) to its proud perfection in the late archaic period (No. 34, Checklist no. 156). The specialist in regional styles will be delighted by the pointed aryballos (Checklist no. 6) and olpe (Checklist no. 5) from Corinth, the two cups made in eastern Greece (Checklist nos. 21 and 22), the hydria from the territory of Chalkis (Checklist no. 14), and the small Laconian cup (No. 2, Checklist no. 17). Those who know their Greek mythology only from Bulfinch or other watered-down versions will be amazed at the vigor and freshness the ancient painters brought to these stories: he will see the Calydonian boar hunt through the eyes of an archaic artist (No. 11, Checklist no. 83) and watch the exodus of Anchises and his family from Troy as depicted five centuries before Vergil (Checklist no. 44) or the death of Aias as painted years before it was dramatized by Sophokles (No. 30, Checklist no. 152). Those less keen on puzzling out depictions of often complex myths will recognize unexpected intimate glances into the home life of the Athenians: women descending into the wine cellar for an unobserved quick drink (No. 39, Checklist no. 138); boys at school confronted by their teachers (cover and No. 34, Checklist no. 156); revels and their consequences (Nos. 32, 33; Checklist nos. 146, 158, 159). Equally impressive to some will be the array of great names in vase painting: the black-figure masters are represented by Lydos (No. 5, Checklist no. 25) and the Affecter (Nos. 6 and 7; Checklist nos. 31 and 37); the inside of a cup attributed to Oltos is painted in black-figure, while the scene on the outside is executed in the new red-figure technique (No. 26, Checklist no. 143), and the style is continued through Epiktetos (No. 29, Checklist no. 145) to the Brygos Painter (No. 30, Checklist no. 152), Makron (No. 33, Checklist no. 158), and Douris (No. 34, Checklist no. 156) to list only the chief of the cup painters. Among the others, the Berlin Painter (Nos. 21 and 22, Checklist nos. 97 and 114), the Eucharides Painter (No. 24, Checklist no. 112), Myson (Checklist no. 102), and the Triptolemos Painter (Checklist no. 100) should be noted in passing. The subtle change in drawing that sheds the archaic manner and leads on to the freedom of the classic period is best exemplified by the fragments of a large hydria with the arming of Achilles, perhaps by the

Hector Painter (Checklist no. 117), and the full classic style is reached with the mug by the Eretria Painter (No. 42, Checklist no. 123). At that time, Attic vase painting went into a decline, and for good drawing we must turn to the red-figure styles formed in southern Italy after the Peloponnesian Wars by the Greek immigrants. By now, however, wall and easel painting were fully developed, and vase painting occupied a humbler position. Whereas in the archaic period, as we know from some rare surviving examples, wall paintings and panel paintings looked remarkably like contemporary vase paintings, the discrepancy in scale between the two, not to mention the more imaginative use of color employed on walls and panels, must have resulted in ever-widening differences. Painting on clay remained dependent on the limited palette of ceramic colors, and though the *drawing*, with its increased understanding of perspective, both corporeal and spatial, with its skilled use of shading, its staggered compositions, and its subtler renderings of facial expressions, must have been similar in the two branches of painting, the overall effect must have been completely different. In the fourth century, especially in the Greek colonies of southern Italy and Sicily, the lavish use of added colors was surely prompted by an understandable desire to rival the bigger paintings on walls and panels, but the result was no closer to "free" painting than, let us say, colored woodcuts or lithographs are to oil paintings.

In their efforts to reproduce the achievements of a more successful branch of painting, the South Italian vase painters concentrated on the pictures and paid less attention to the special requirements of the different shapes, with the result that the pictures tend to lose their close, organic relationship with the surface on which they are painted. In turn, the potters' repertory, which included the traditional Attic shapes as well as some specifically native ones, lost the subtle sense of proportions and careful balance of component parts that distinguished the Athenian prototypes. It has therefore been said with some justice that South Italian vase painting can best be appreciated on fragments. Here the eye is not distracted by the shape and can read, as it were, the drawing in all its purity. Significantly, Mr. Bareiss's forays into South Italian wares have been concentrated on fragments (Nos. 43, 44, and 45; Checklist nos. 223, 221, and 205).

The exhibition spans more than a thousand years of vase painting, from a delightful miniature stirrup jar of ca. 1300 B.C. (Checklist no. 1) to the molded wares of Augustan Rome dated in the late first century B.C. (No. 47, Checklist no. 253). It focuses, however, on the seventh to the middle of the fourth centuries B.C. In the history of Greece, it is these three centuries, in which Greek culture was born and flourished, in which her achievements in all fields—architecture, sculpture, painting, literature, music, rhetoric, philosophy, science, and politics—came to pass. This exhibition, small and restricted as it is, puts into sharp focus much of the Greek heritage, fortunately not yet forgotten.

DIETRICH VON BOTHMER

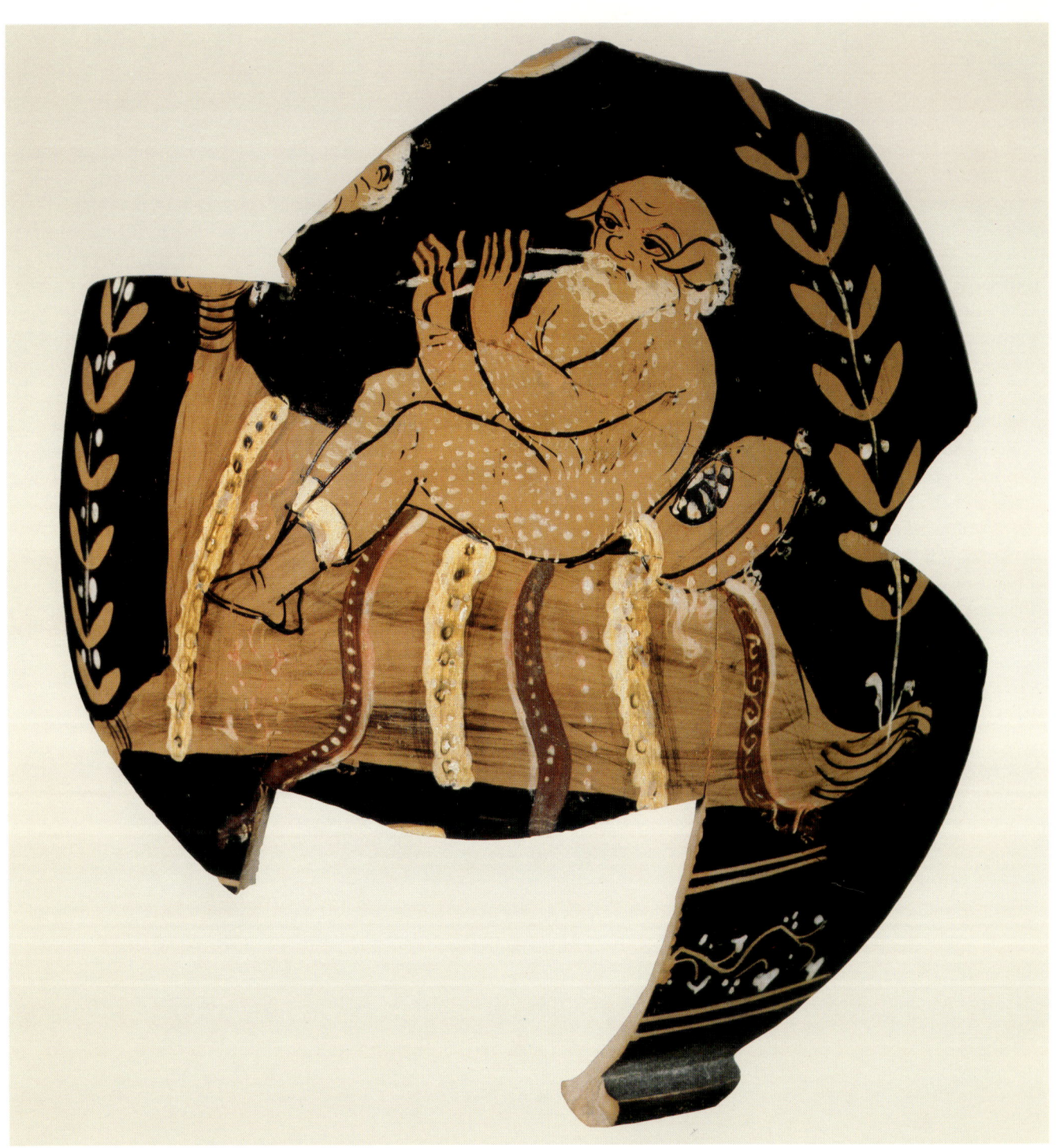

THE WORLD OF GREEK VASES

Ancient Greek vases offer us, as they did the Greeks, many pleasures. Products of excellent craftsmanship, the shapes appeal to us as models of the potter's art. Simple ornamental and floral patterns or rows of animals represented by accomplished draughtsmanship please us with decorative beauty; and in the best figural representations, the drawing reaches a level of art equal to the supreme works of Greek sculpture. Finally, the scenes represented can be seen as illustrations of Greek mythology and various aspects of Greek life.

This last perspective, the study of the subjects, or iconography, has been the traditional approach to the study of Greek vases. The gods and heroes, familiar to us not only from classical literature and monuments but also from Western art and thought since the Renaissance, appear on vases as the living presences they were in the youth of humanity which was Hellas. In combination with ancient literature, the images of Greek art (to which vases contribute the major part) provide a better understanding of the myths and of their evolution and meaning for the Greeks. They even provide evidence for the nature of theatrical productions and poetry based on myths.

Mythological scenes on vases are often hard to distinguish from representations of daily life. The ancient Greeks lacked the historical approach widespread only since the nineteenth century. Thus, the narrative images on vases do not present the actual settings of Greek prehistory where most of the mythological tales originate. Rather the arms and armor, furniture, sports, music, and festivities of the gods and heroes are those of archaic and classical Greece. The immortals recline on couches and drink from vessels of the artist's time.

Often, the role of mythology was instructive. Even though full citizens were a minority in the Greek city states, the human condition there provided more freedom than the Near Eastern kingdoms. Freedom of thought within the context of a commonly accepted morality and explanation of the universe inspired competition in all kinds of creative activity, including most of the visual arts. Mythology as a sylloge of popular fairy tales and patriotic legends provided many generations with ideal types that could serve as measures for the athletes, warriors, youths, and citizens. The visual arts helped to establish this tradition of mythology by reflecting in their compositions the ideals and thoughts of their own Greek communities. Thus, the mirror of mythology demonstrated that the Greeks were, in a sense, "Platonists" long before Plato, as they placed "ideas" and prototypes before real things.

Belonging by their nature to the minor arts, vases sometimes reflect in their drawings monumental sculpture or lost wall paintings. At their best, they are great art in themselves. Attic vases from the late sixth and early fifth centuries B.C. can be compared with the drawings of the best masters from the Renaissance to modern times. One must forget that the surface is curved and focus on the composition as a two-dimensional creation.

Although these drawings may look very much alike to the uninitiated eye, they often express the unique characters of identifiable artists whose careers can be traced, sometimes through decades. Scholarly research in Greek vase painting started in the last century. The main work was done by a single remarkable man, Sir John Beazley, C.H. (1885–1970), Lincoln Professor of Art and Archaeology at Oxford University. Beazley spent most of the time between 1910 and his death identifying vase painters. He attributed some 50,000 Attic vases from the sixth, fifth, and fourth centuries B.C. to different hands. Yet he also found time to lay the framework for the study of Italiote (Greek vases from South Italy) and Etruscan painted vases. His method was the perception of style and the analysis of the individuality of the draughtsman. Thanks to his phenomenal memory and sensitivity, he perceived not only the style of each painter but also his chronological evolution. Later, Beazley's conclusions were often confirmed by joins between sherds found in museums and collections widely separated in distance. The most famous example is a cup by the painter Oltos now spread among the museums in Rome, Florence, Heidelberg, Braunschweig, Baltimore, and Bowdoin College.

Beazley's many other important contributions concern mythology, Greek and Roman literature, and vase inscriptions, as he was a very fine classicist and accomplished philologist. He was not just a great scholar, he was a great man as well, a model of kindness and integrity, always ready to help, always improving himself. Those who had the privilege to know him cannot forget him; he was truly a hero among mortals. Beazley had a special connection with the Bareiss vases. He provided many attributions, and, in his later years, he advised Walter Bareiss whenever called upon.

Few vase painters are known by their real names, as vases are only occasionally signed. Two types of signatures occur: "so and so made (me)" and "so and so drew (me)." While the latter refers unequivocally to the artist who really did the painting with his hands, the former may sometimes refer to the owner of the pottery shop, at other times to the actual potting craftsman. Potters who are known by name also provide names for painters who are otherwise anonymous. Thus, the Brygos Painter is the leading artist in the workshop of the potter who signed himself Brygos. Other painters were named, primarily by Beazley, after their subject matter, after the name of a beautiful boy whom they praise on their vases, or after a museum or collector who preserves one or more of their works.

Although today we are attracted essentially by the painting on Greek vases, the Greeks seem to have appreciated equally the firm hand of the potter who turned the elegant shapes with well-balanced proportions. The painter not only respected but also enhanced the tectonic qualities of the vase with the decoration, disposing the ornamental patterns and figures in harmony with the shape. This process recalls the composition of music or the sophisticated construction of Greek architecture. Perfect articulation, a Greek virtue *par excellence,* is seen in the interrelationship of lip, neck, body, stem, and foot. The placement of the handles determines the sides, front, and back of the vase.

The shapes created by ancient potters deserve separate attention. The names given to vase shapes in the nineteenth century derive from Greek sources, but only in a few cases are they actually the names used to designate that shape of vase in antiquity. The hydria, for example, was the three-handled vase used to carry water. But many other names exist in ancient writings which seem to have been interchangeable for various forms, much as we use mug or cup to describe many variations of one shape. However, four basic kinds of Greek vases can be distinguished: drinking vessels (kylikes, kotylai, skyphoi, kantharoi), mixing vessels (primarily various types of kraters), storage containers (amphorae, hydriai, pelikai), and smaller utensils (lekythoi, jugs, and oinochoai).

Vases were thrown from well-matured, carefully prepared clay just as today. When a pot had dried to the "leather-hard" state, the painter first covered it with a fine ochre slip called miltos, which gives the reserved areas their characteristic shiny reddish-orange color. With a metallic point or wooden stick, perhaps charcoal, the artist made a preliminary sketch on the surface of the vase. A large brush was then used to trace the broad, flat contours of the figures and ornamental patterns and also to fill all the black background. Finally came the delicate procedure of drawing the fine relief lines, not only to provide the inner details but very often, at least in the archaic period, to highlight the basic contours of the composition. What instrument and procedure was used to create the raised relief line is still uncertain. Some details, such as the hair, were done with thicker, standard brushes. Finally, delicate indications of muscles or other anatomy, special materials like fur or tortoise shell, and sometimes drapery folds were carefully added in dilute glaze.

Because of the nature of the "glaze" he was using, the painter could not see his composition well. Not a true glaze in the modern sense, his paint was actually the finest refined clay that had risen to the top of the potting clay in the settling beds, somewhat richer in iron than the lower strata. This highly refined clay was then mixed with fine ash and probably animal manure containing some albumen to keep the particles in suspension and to prevent sedimentation. Thus, before firing, the glaze was a thick, greenish liquid which could not have smelled very fragrant.

The lustrous black color was actually achieved by a complex firing process finally understood in the 1940's. First, a high-temperature firing stage hardened the pot to a new consistency. Next, a reducing stage in an atmosphere poor in oxygen and rich in carbon monoxide converted the red iron oxide in the clay to another type of iron oxide which was black in color. In this stage, the glaze formed a fine, nonporous black surface. Finally, in a short period of exposure to an oxidizing fire, unglazed areas of the pot returned to reddish-orange.

In the ancient world, the finely decorated Attic vases were appreciated much as the finest porcelain is today, as rather luxurious products and not everyday ware. But the same potters who manufactured these vases also turned out common ceramics. The symposion is one of the Greek festivities for which fine vases must have been used if we can judge by the very slight indications of wear on some cups, kraters, and psykters. It seems, though, that many of the best vases were made for export to the colonies in southern Italy and to Etruria, there often to be used primarily for funerary purposes or as precious offerings made in the sanctuaries of the gods.

A short overview of the history of Greek vases must begin in the dawn of the Bronze Age. Very attractive multicolor vases were produced in the earliest periods; but later in the second millennium, before 1200, the vases became less substantial, the decoration rude and simple. However, several technical advances were transmitted to the Greeks of the early Iron Age—the preparation of the clay, the potter's wheel, the use of the kiln with three stages of firing resulting in the black "glaze." With this knowledge, the Greeks of the tenth century began to produce an elegant pottery called Geometric because of the nature of its decoration. Athens was the best-known center for production of these vases. In the eighth century, animals and even stylized human figures appeared, often representing aspects of the funeral such as the laying out of the body, mourning, and games in honor of the dead man.

While Athenian ceramics were made primarily for local consumption, the vases of the more developed centers of the seventh century, like Corinth or the southwest coast of Asia Minor and its adjacent islands, began to produce vases as a trade commodity for markets all over the Greek world, including the colonies of southwest Italy and Sicily. Characteristic of this period is a change in decoration. Floral patterns were introduced into the ornamental vocabulary and rows of animals, perhaps inspired by woven fabrics, appear frequently. Corinth specialized in fine drinking cups and exquisite oil containers, thousands of which survive today.

Corinthian vase painters also initiated a new method of decoration called black-figure. The figures of animals were done in silhouette with incised details and added colors. But with the beginning of the sixth century B.C., the Corinthian potters found a new rival in the products from Athens. During the earlier sixth century, the Athenians were still learning from Corinthian vases in shapes, patterns, and figurative compositions. Before mid-century they had overcome their competitors. To regain their stronghold on the market, the Corinthians even tried to imitate the newly-favored Athenian figurative style, but the effort was futile.

A distinguishing feature of the Attic black-figure vases was the introduction in the decoration of narrative scenes. During the second half of the century, the best masters of the black-figure style, even the greatest of all, Exekias, exploited the technique to its limits. By the end of the sixth century, the possibilities of black-figure had been exhausted, though the technique continued to be used in some minor workshops for another half century; and a new direction was found after a period of experimentation. Instead of making the figures in silhouette, artists tried leaving them the color of the vase (reserved), and emphasized their contours by surrounding them with a black background, thus creating red-figure. Before the end of the sixth century, this new technique had reached maturity, and in the first three decades of the fifth century, one masterpiece after another was produced by the workshops of Athens. The zenith was followed by a slow decline, but even in the mid-fourth century some handsome vases were still being produced by Athenian potters. However, the creative fire had been extinguished in Athens, and a new spark began in the centers of South Italy (in the areas of today's Campania, around Taranto, and in Sicily), perhaps in workshops employing emigré Athenian potters and painters. The end of the fourth century marked the end of decorated figurative pottery, replaced by attempts to produce polychromed, multi-colored ware in South Italy and Sicily. The Greek vase had attained its classical height and disappeared.

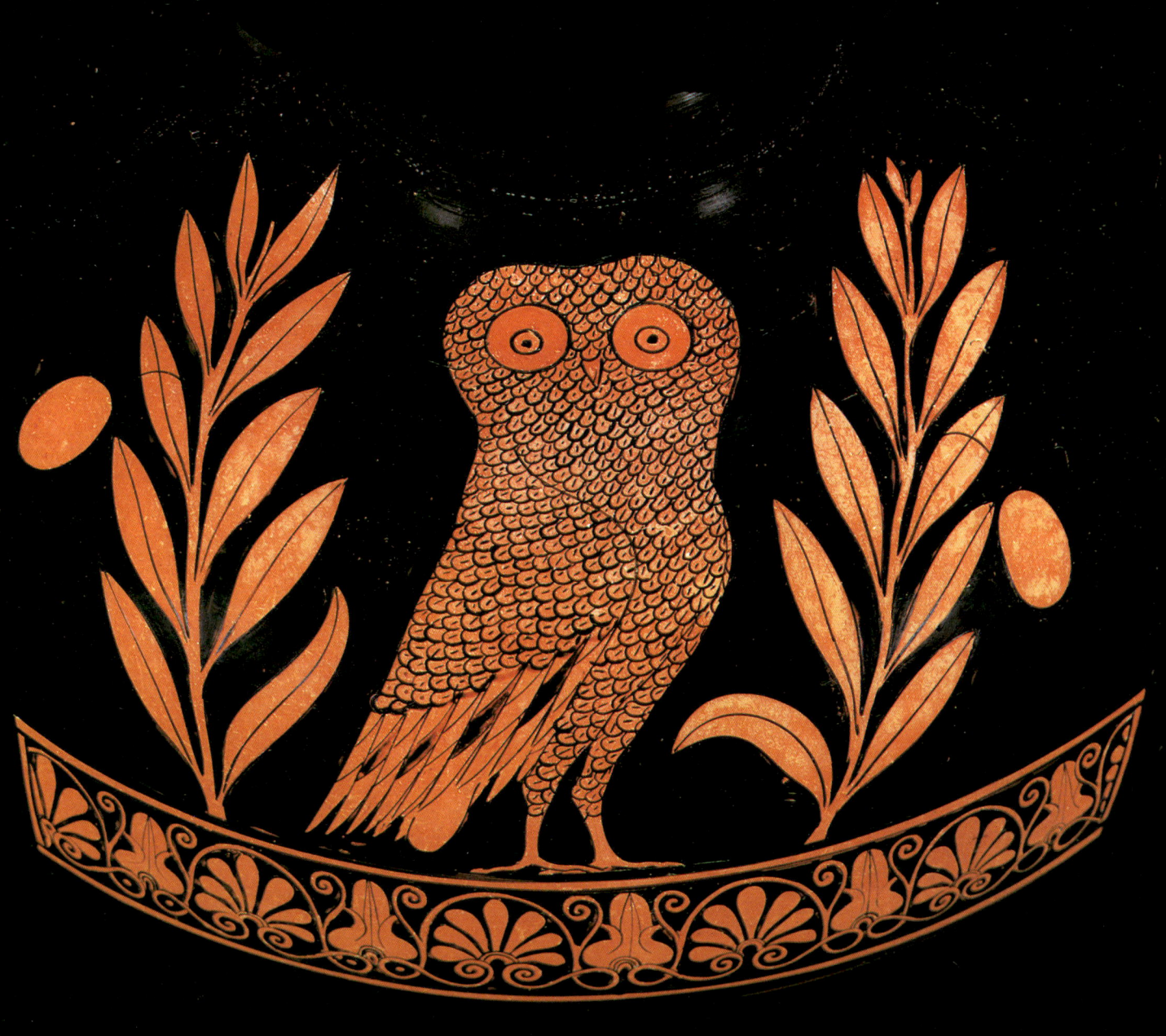

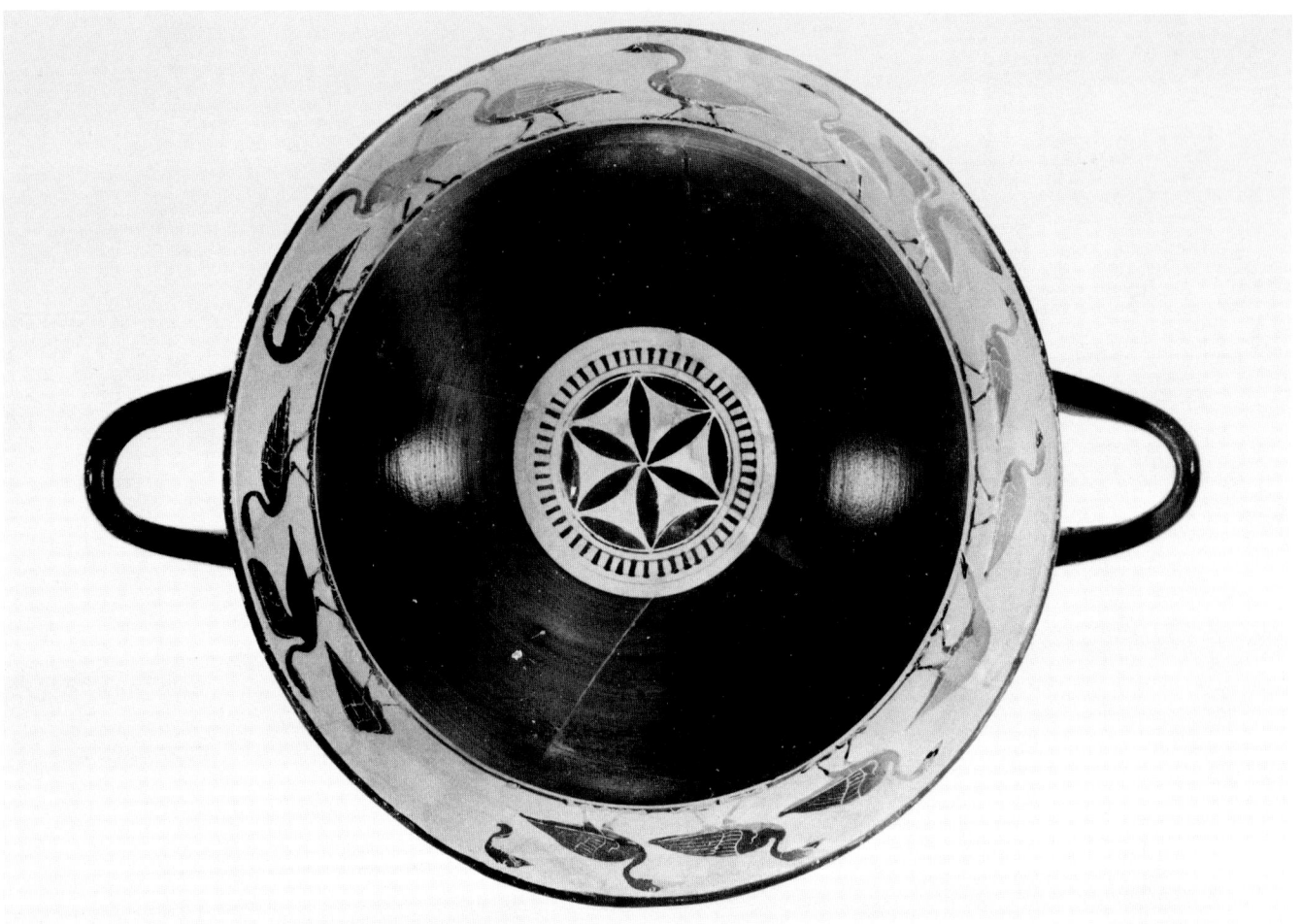

1. East Greek Lip Cup
Circa 530 B.C.
Height: 9.3 cm.
Diameter: 14.2 cm.
Checklist no. 22.

This shape of kylix is a parallel to the Attic Little Master lip cups (see Nos. 12 and 13). The potting is, however, more delicate; and the decoration follows the conventions of East Greece (the west coast of Asia Minor and Aegean islands, inhabited by Greek-speaking peoples from the Bronze Age onward) in the choice of motifs and their disposition. The deep bowl of the cup is the traditional and proper shape to be filled with wine: it is painted all black, with a geometric rosette on the bottom. The lip represents a kind of shore to this pool of the "wine dark sea," thus the waterbirds that parade around it in various stances are a pleasant but natural conceit. Waterbirds are a well-established motif on East Greek drinking bowls, known since the Geometric period. The cup provides welcome evidence that, even under the undoubted preeminence of Attic workshops in the later sixth century, the production of good quality Greek ceramics was still going on in other local workshops.

2. Laconian Cup
Attributed to the Hunt Painter
Circa 540 B.C.
Height: 8.8 cm.
Diameter: 11.8 cm.
Checklist no. 17.

The standard image of Sparta is one of military barracks with iron discipline; but in the archaic period, the arts and crafts flourished in Sparta as in every other Greek city. Of course, the full Spartan citizen would have despised sitting at a potters' wheel; but there was a large population of free workmen in Sparta who produced excellent painted vases, appreciated and exported even to the Greek colonies in Italy, although to a lesser extent than the more highly prized Corinthian or Attic wares.

Laconian cups are particularly appealing to our modern eyes. The decoration is often very plain, as on the Bareiss cup. The outside is painted with only simple patterns, but it includes the judicious use of added red. Inside, the tondo shows a lion looking over its back. The painter did not try to represent the majesty of the wild beast. He could scarcely have seen a real lion. Instead, he employed the standard heraldic schema current on Corinthian vases, developing it to make a pleasant decoration.

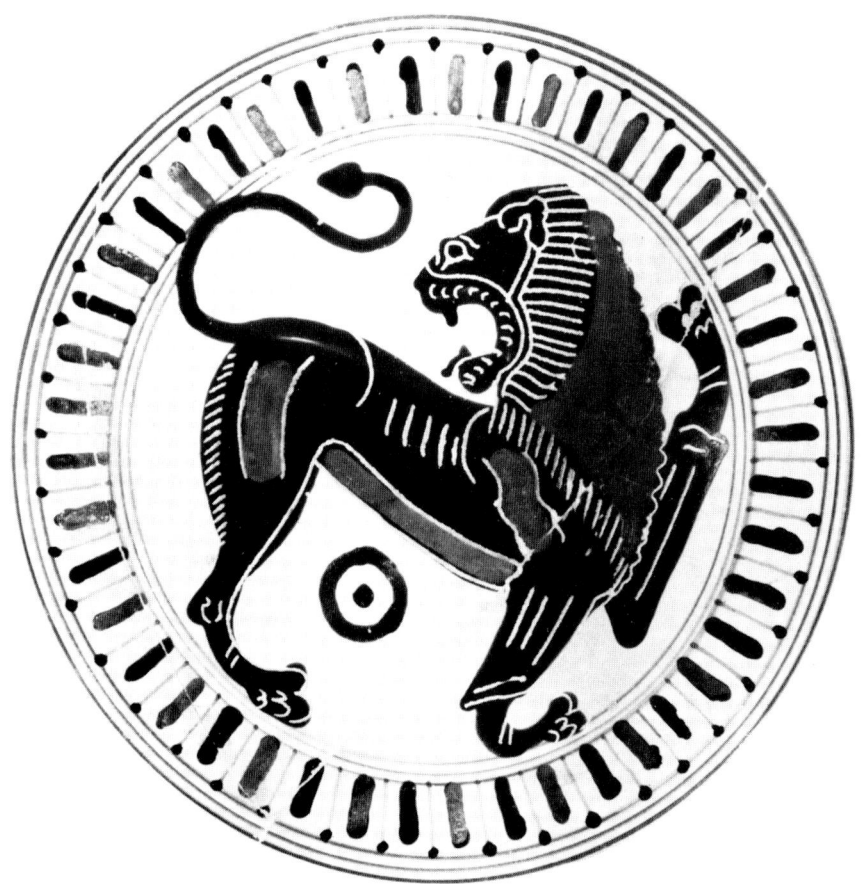

3. Chalcidian Cup
Attributed to the Phineus Painter
Circa 530 B.C.
Height: 10.6 cm.
Diameter: 26 cm.
Checklist no. 15.

The shape is as elegant as the decoration is simple. The potter threw a deep cup with a large foot, a shape soon imitated by Attic ceramicists. The artist painted ears, eyes, and a nose on both sides in a very stylized pattern. In classical Greek traditions, as in the folklore of other countries and times, eyes had an apotropaic meaning—protection against all kinds of magical spells and dangers, and especially against the evil eye. On a drinking cup, such protection is particularly important: the drinker cannot see what is happening around him, and the painted eyes watch for any foul play that might occur. The original magical function was certainly still appreciated in the late sixth century B.C. when this cup was made; but at the same time, people must have appreciated the purely decorative effect more and more, for the eyes appear on other vase shapes as well (see the amphora, No. 9).

4. Euboean Neck Amphora
Circa 570-560 B.C.
Height: 35.5 cm.
Checklist no. 18.

The potters of the island of Euboea were so strongly inspired by Attic workshops that only recently have their products been clearly identified. This neck amphora from the second quarter of the sixth century could easily be confused with contemporary Attic vases, so similar are the potting, the pattern decoration, and even the figure types. However, the clay is slightly different; and the painter, who decorated another amphora in the Bareiss collection (Checklist no. 19), has a personality quite distinct from his Attic contemporaries. He enjoys the decorative effect of added colors and the ornament in general.

Even the mythological subject the artist has chosen for the main zone of the obverse is less a narrative than a pleasant decoration. Hermes is shown introducing the three goddesses in the beauty competition to the Trojan prince Paris, but the scene differs greatly from the standard composition presented by Attic painters. The three goddesses cannot be distinguished from one another. They wear the same style of dress, only with different patterns. Hermes, raising the *kerykeion*—the messenger's staff—takes a resolute step forward to shake hands with Paris; Paris is not shown as the youthful Trojan prince-shepherd but as a very well dressed, bearded gentleman. Between Hermes and Paris, an owl looks out of the picture. It is purely decorative, an animal drawn with pleasure but with no more significance than the lions, rooster, and sirens in the lower zone. No interpretation can be proposed for the two bearded men in conversation between two sphinxes in the main zone of the reverse. Only loosely constrained by the requirements of the narrative, the painter is free to be inventive without pedantry.

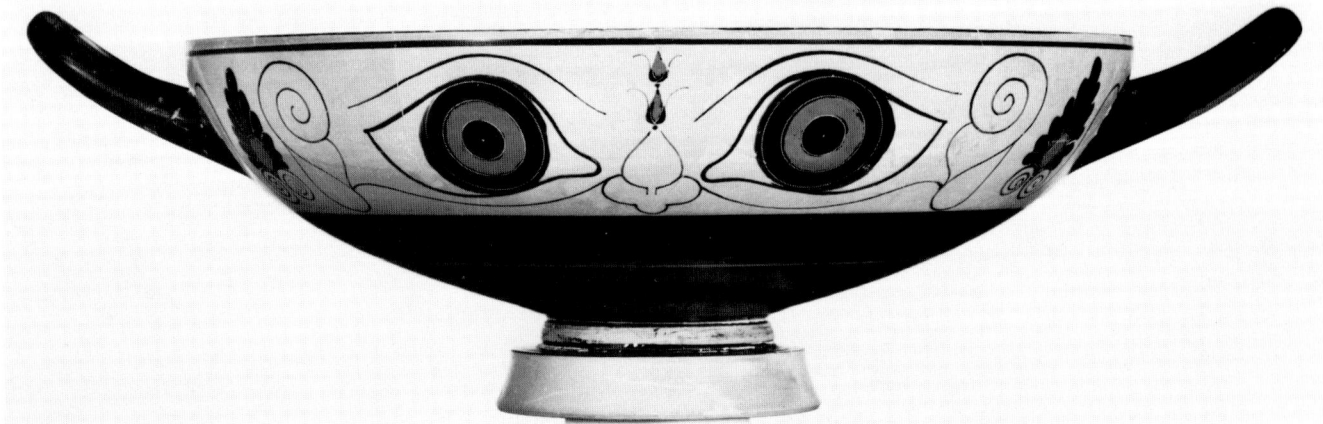

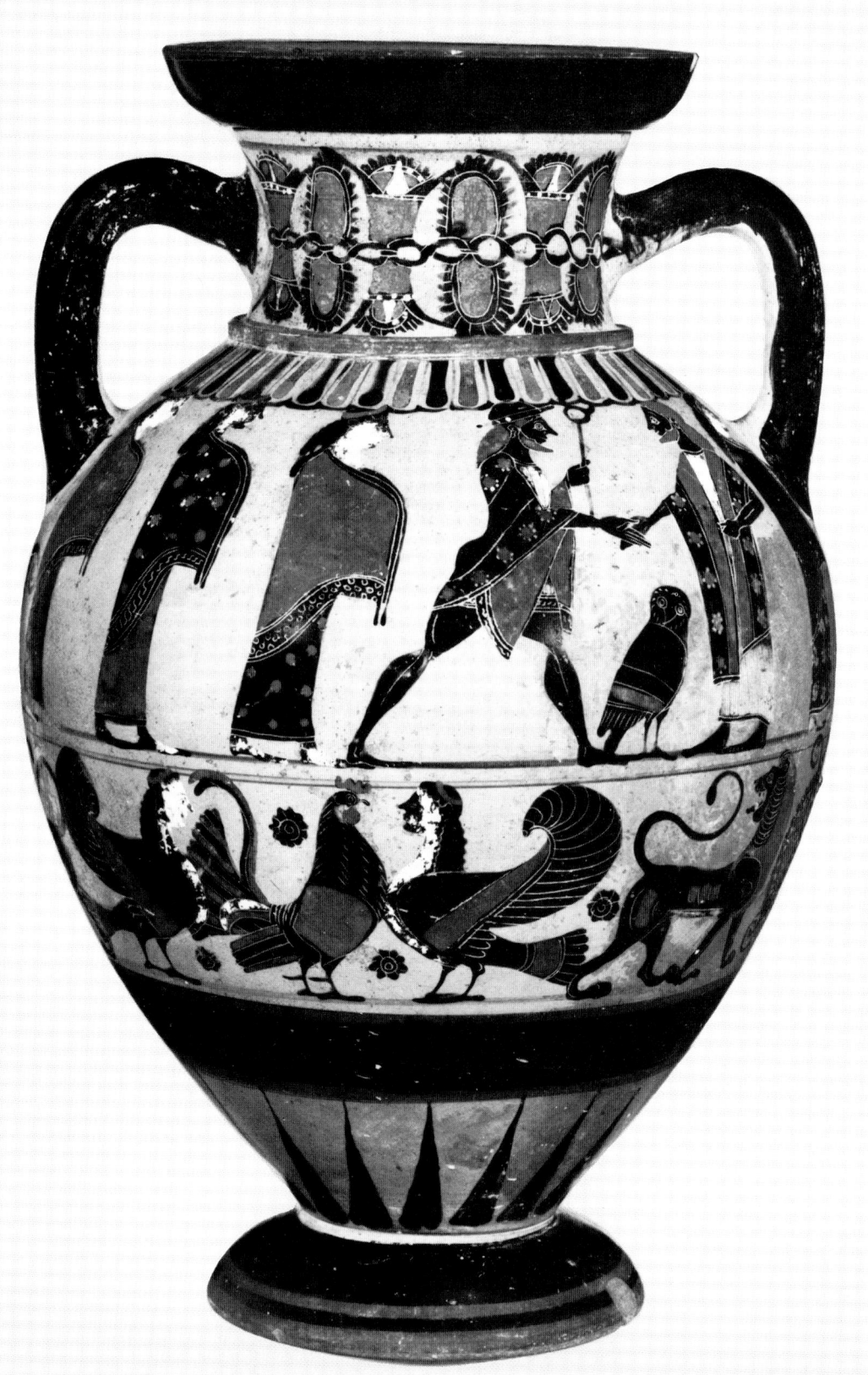

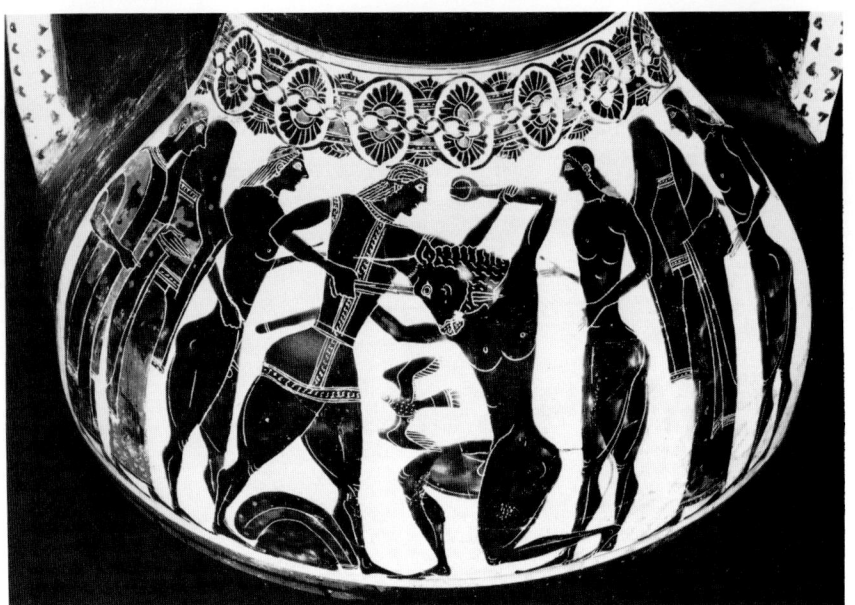

5. Amphora Type A
Attributed to Lydos, or someone close to him
Circa 550-540 B.C.
Height: 45.7 cm.
Checklist no. 25.

Theseus is killing the Minotaur. He moves with purposeful dignity, his helmet set on the ground between his feet. The monster has fallen on one knee as the sword pierces his neck. Theseus grasps the Minotaur's left wrist and his victory is complete, to the joy of the Athenian youths and maidens who view the spectacle. Instead of being devoured by the Minotaur as they expected, they attend his slaying. The story—a favorite in Athens since it involved the city's national hero—is told with gusto, without superfluous emphasis on decorative effect. However, several details are recorded with great care, like every feature on the beautiful bull's head of the Minotaur and the precise lines and decoration of the peploi and mantles of the two girls. Three of the four youths are nude; and they look like contemporary statues of *kouroi*: with long, carefully dressed hair and the muscular chests, narrow waists, and powerful buttocks and thighs of trained athletes. There is just one purely ornamental filler element: the eagle between the two protagonists. The lively scene presents an eloquent contrast to the same subject in the purely stylized conception of the Affecter (No. 7).

On the secondary side, the painter has represented the homecoming of two young riders who are welcomed by an elderly man and two women. Behind the horses stands a nude groom. Perhaps they are the Dioskouroi, but even if not, the painter communicates quite clearly the story of their arrival.

6. One-piece (Belly) Amphora, Type C
Attributed to the Affecter Painter
Potted by the same artist
Circa 530 B.C.
Height: 38.7 cm.
Checklist no. 31.

About the middle of the sixth century B.C., an idiosyncratic personality appeared in Attic vase production. He seems to have learned his art from Amasis, a well-established potter and painter who united in his drawings a keen understanding for telling a story with an accomplished sense for decoration. It is especially this decorative sensibility that distinguishes the work of the artist we call the Affecter Painter. Like his master, the Affecter painted the vases he threw himself. The proof that both were done by one and the same man lies in the fact that the vases and the drawings are penetrated by the same spirit, which is rather contrary to the main trend of Greek art. The craftsmanship is outstanding. The vases, as thin as eggshells, are perfectly thrown; and the drawing is executed with finesse. But, contrary to the main preoccupation of contemporary potters, the Affecter's shapes quite intentionally neglect articulation, and at first glance they seem out of proportion.

This is the case with the one-piece amphora in the Bareiss collection. Indisputably elegant, the shape looks a little odd, as does the drawing. The main side shows a bearded old man, wearing a chiton and mantle, extending his arm towards a naked man who is running away and looking backwards. They are framed by two nude spectators who gesture emphatically. This is clearly a variant of a subject common in Attic vase painting since before the middle of the sixth century, an elderly lover courting a youth. However, the Affecter has introduced some variations. The first deviation from the orthodox rendering of the subject is that the beloved one is bearded. The second is that all the emphatic gestures appear devoid of content; the whole scene is a contrived decoration, vacant of meaning. The other side seems to present the same approach to its subject. Here, framed by two draped dignitaries, the two protagonists are represented as if they are running. In fact, no suggestion of real movement is intended. The position of the legs, like the theatrical position of the hands, upraised with the thumbs separated from the fingers, serves no other purpose than to achieve a perfect composition. As is always the case with the Affecter, one has the impression that, while achieving a polished piece of *l'art pour l'art,* he mocks the well-established repertory of Attic vase painting.

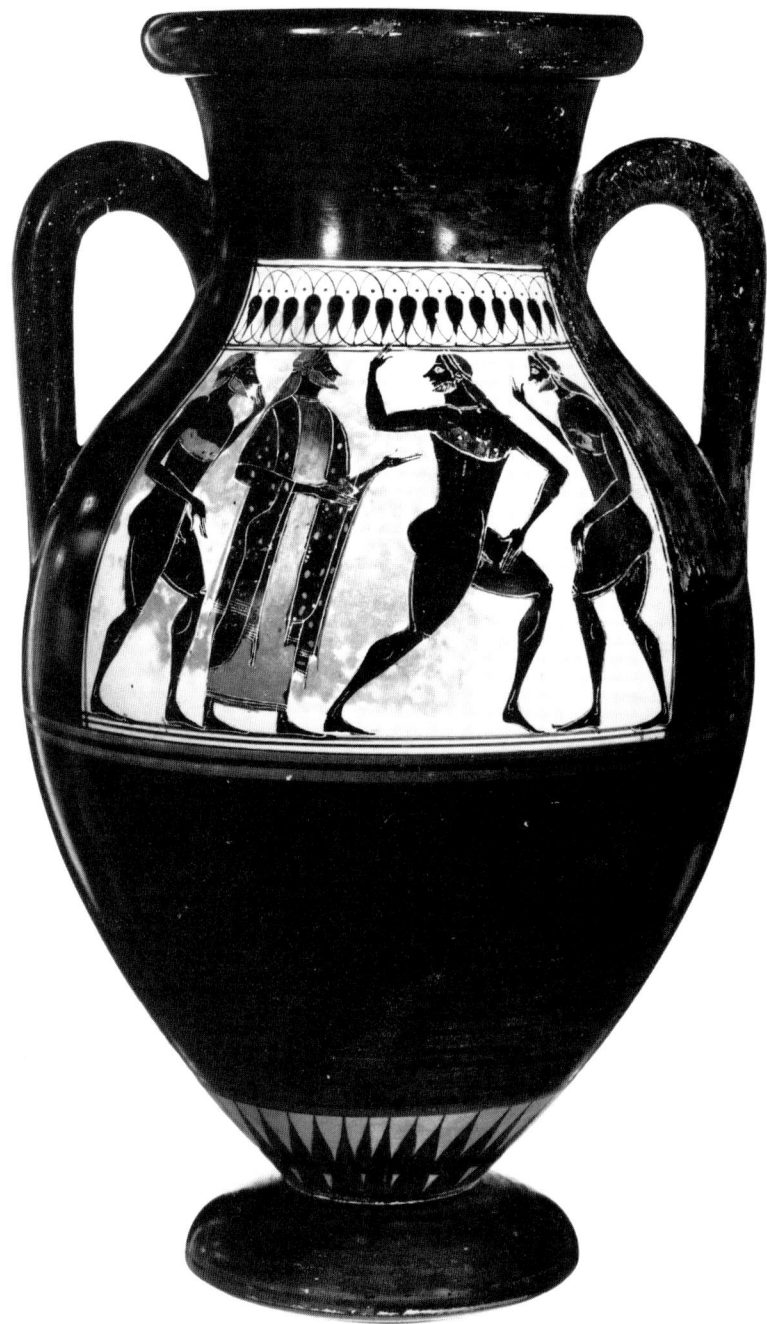

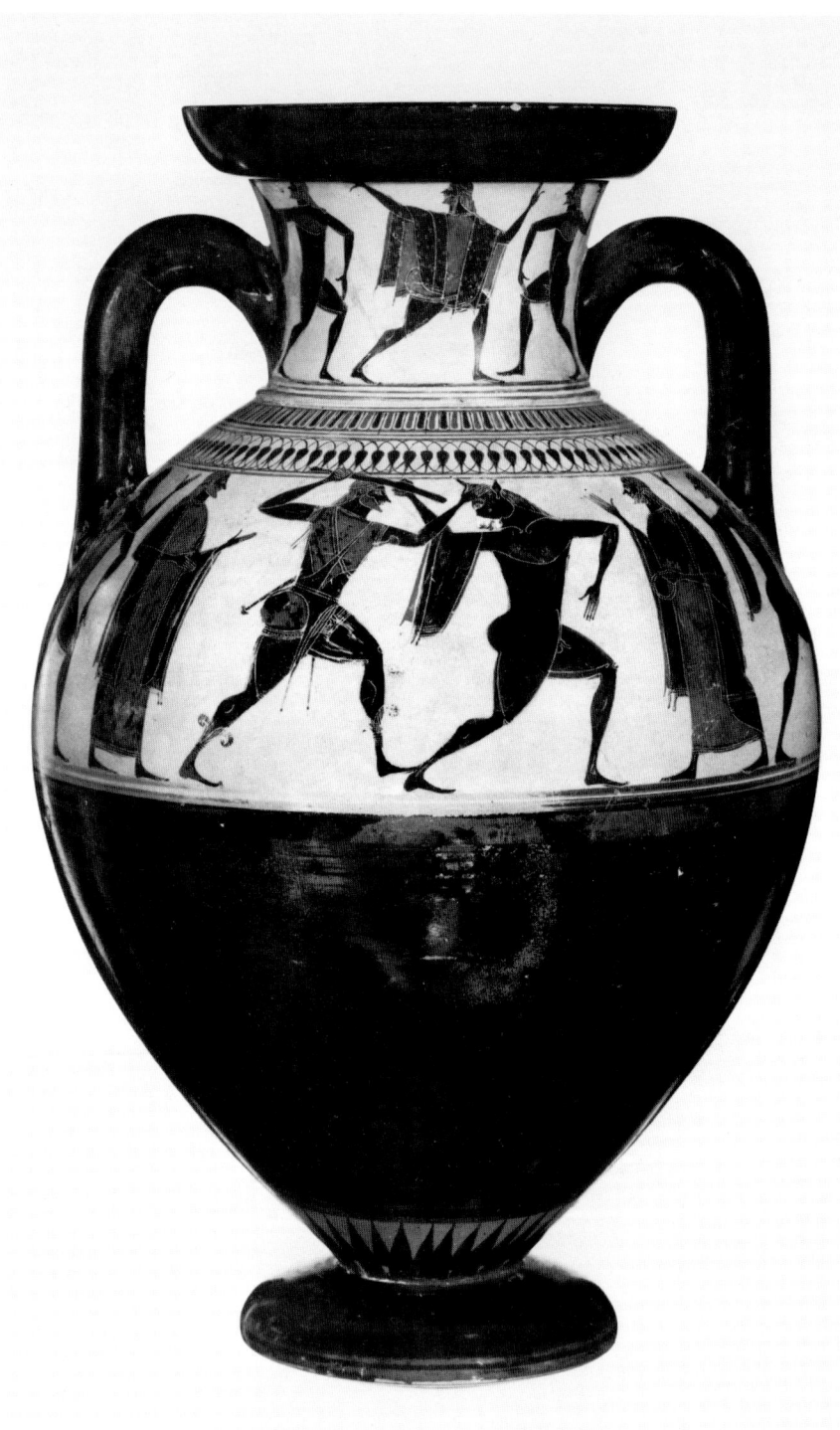

7. Neck Amphora
Attributed to the Affecter Painter
Potted by the same artist
Before 530 B.C.
Height: 39 cm.
Checklist no. 37.

The Affecter limited his production mostly to one-piece and neck amphorae. The neck amphora shape quite naturally involves strong articulation between neck and shoulder, and the Affecter further separates the neck from the body with a raised plastic ring. His particular approach to the articulation, however, succeeds in rejecting the traditions of Attic pottery, perhaps even more than with his one-piece amphorae. The body of this neck amphora appears like a beautiful, swelling ovoid form, carried by a finely molded foot which is as independent as the superimposed neck, although, taken as a whole, the profile of the vase gives a fluid impression.

The unusual also occurs in the decoration of the vase. On the obverse of the Bareiss amphora's neck is a bearded man wearing a short mantle (*chlamys*) and running to the right; he looks backward with his arms upraised. He is framed by two nude men moving about energetically but aimlessly. On the reverse of the neck, a nude youth runs as if towards the bearded man of the obverse. The *chlamys* of the youth is intentionally cut into two pieces, each of which hangs from an elbow, against all logic: the Affecter is evidently stating openly his disdain for reality. In fact, the two sides look rather like a traditional courting scene cut in two with some underlying irony. The general impression is that of a ballet without any meaning.

The subjects represented on the body are well defined and, one could say, complementary: Herakles clubbing a centaur on one side and Theseus clubbing the Minotaur on the other. Yet even here, the painter does not take his subjects too seriously. Herakles caresses the hindquarters of his adversary with a friendly gesture, his left arm represented parallel to the right arm of the centaur raised in supplication, while the centaur's left arm is bent ineffectively down, grasping a stone. Behind the centaur, Iolaos carries his master's bow, preceded by a fawn pressed in between him and a nude spectator. Two other spectators, one in a mantle, the second nude, stand behind Herakles. Two similar pairs frame the scene on the other side, where Theseus seizes the horn of the Minotaur, but the monster firmly grasps Theseus' club. The movements and gestures of the protagonists have no connection with real action; the poses of the other figures are equally mannered. The two scenes are separated by the handles. Yet, these functional attachments actually affect the decoration of the vase because their lower ends are surrounded by elaborate patterns that cut into the figures next to them. A flying bird under one handle and a small cauldron on a high stand beneath the other underline the separation of the two scenes, but the distinction is simultaneously denied by the participants: the second onlooker behind each hero, while correctly moving towards the center, is represented looking back as if more interested in the event on the other side.

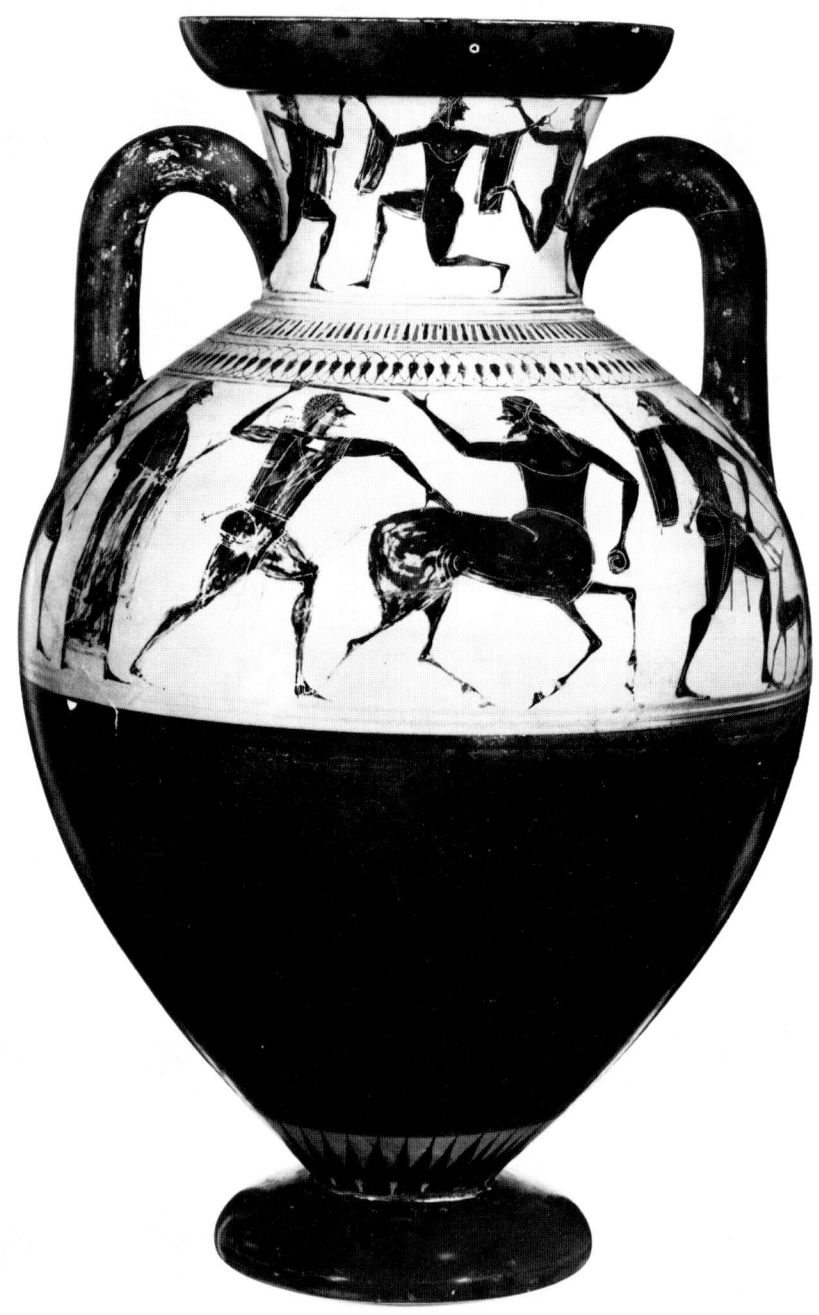

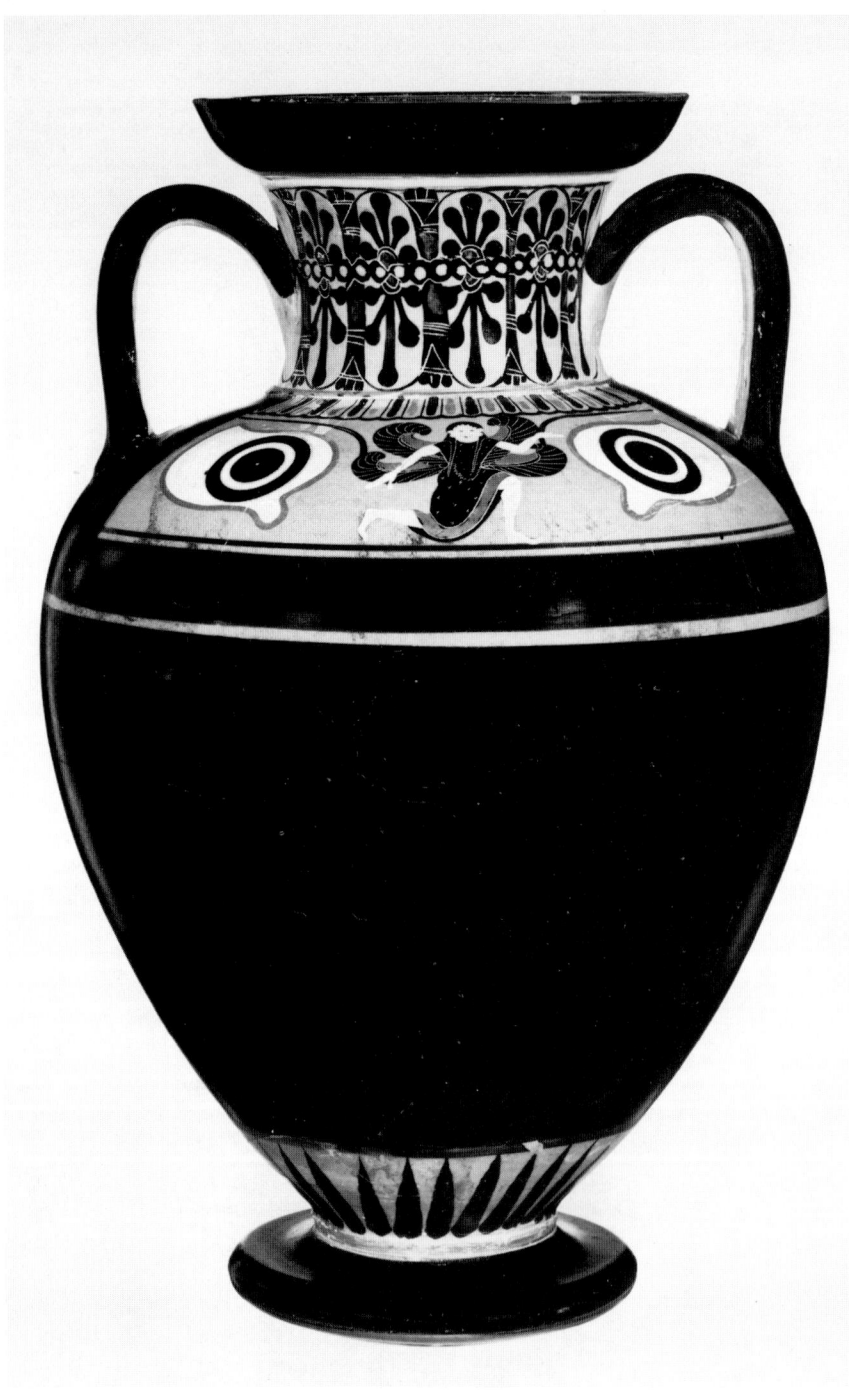

**8. Neck Amphora
Assigned to the Class of Neck
Amphorae with Shoulder Pictures
Circa 530 B.C.
Height: 36.8 cm.
Checklist no. 39.**

This neck amphora is an excellent example of the black-figure technique in its late phase. The potting is competent, and the swell of the large black body is marked by a reserved fillet just before it turns into the shoulder. The painted panel on each side presents a pair of eyes, which no longer pretend to prevent evil as they did on the Chalcidian cup (No. 3) — the eyes are just an effective decorative motif. A winged female figure running with deeply bent knees — the convention used by Greek artists to indicate flight — replaces the nose one would formerly have seen between them (see No. 3). On the main side, the figure is the old-fashioned and apotropaic Gorgo (Medusa) with double wings, a large rounded face, and her tongue protruding between her fangs. The formerly fearsome creature has been reduced to a mostly decorative appearance. On the reverse, a youthful goddess "flies" looking backwards; one would like to call her Nike or Iris, the messenger of the gods, but her identity remains imprecise.

**9. Hydria
Attributed to the Lykomedes
Painter
Circa 510 B.C.
Height (with handle): 40 cm.
Checklist no. 60.**

This vase by the Lykomedes Painter is

a perfect example of the standard black-figure hydria. The distinctive three handles were completely functional—the two horizontal handles for carrying, the long, vertical handle for pouring. The form is strongly articulated, with a wide mouth, columnar neck, flattish shoulder, ovoid body, and disk foot. The rotellae on the sides of the rear handle at the point of attachment to the mouth and the modeled clay "rivets" within the mouth just in front of the handle are proof of a metal prototype for the shape.

On the front, Apollo and Herakles struggle for possession of the Delphic tripod. Apollo's twin, Artemis, stands behind her brother on the left. Athena, the protectress of Herakles, stands on the right in peplos, aegis, and high-crested Attic helmet. Herakles was driven to madness by the jealousy of Hera and murdered his first wife and children. Guilty of blood crimes, he sought refuge and cleansing at the shrine of Apollo in Delphi. Unfortunately, Apollo was away at the time, so Herakles questioned the Pythia, the Delphic oracle, as to how to cure his sickness. She had no answer, and the angry hero decided to steal the tripod which stood in the temple. The god returned and struggled with Herakles for the tripod. Finally Zeus intervened; and Herakles was punished for his crimes with enslavement to Eurystheus, king of Tiryns, who then devised the famous twelve labors. On the shoulder is one of these labors, Herakles wrestling the Nemean lion, while Iolaos, Athena, and Hermes look on.

The artist, so-called for the charioteer of Apollo whose name is inscribed on his krater in New York,

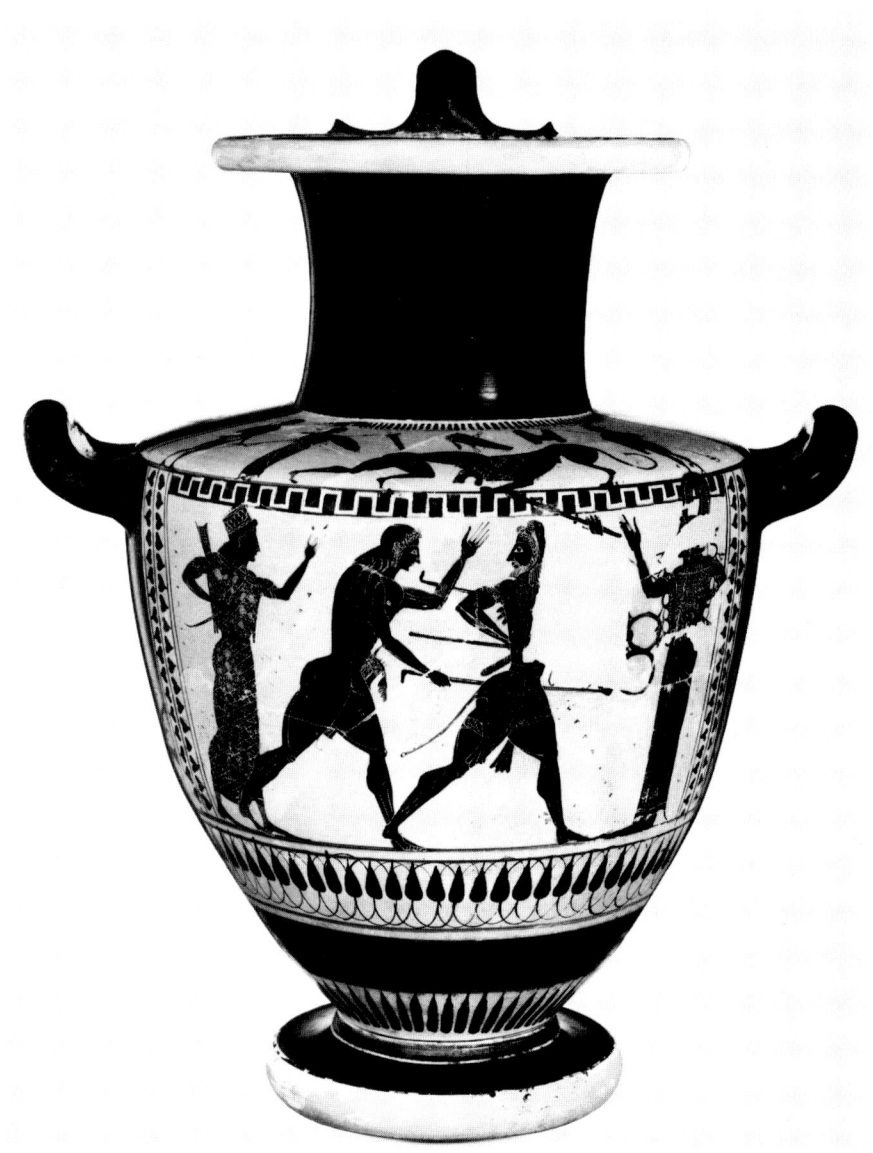

illustrates the end of a tradition. He chose to continue using the dying black-figure technique at the time when red-figure artists were experimenting with all sorts of interesting new possibilities. His figures are elegant, even over-refined, and they lack the vitality found among the works of his adventuresome red-figure contemporaries like Euthymides and Euphronios. The Lykomedes Painter's one concession to progress is the use of white slip on the edges of the mouth and the foot to accentuate two prominent parts of the vase profile, the top and the bottom.

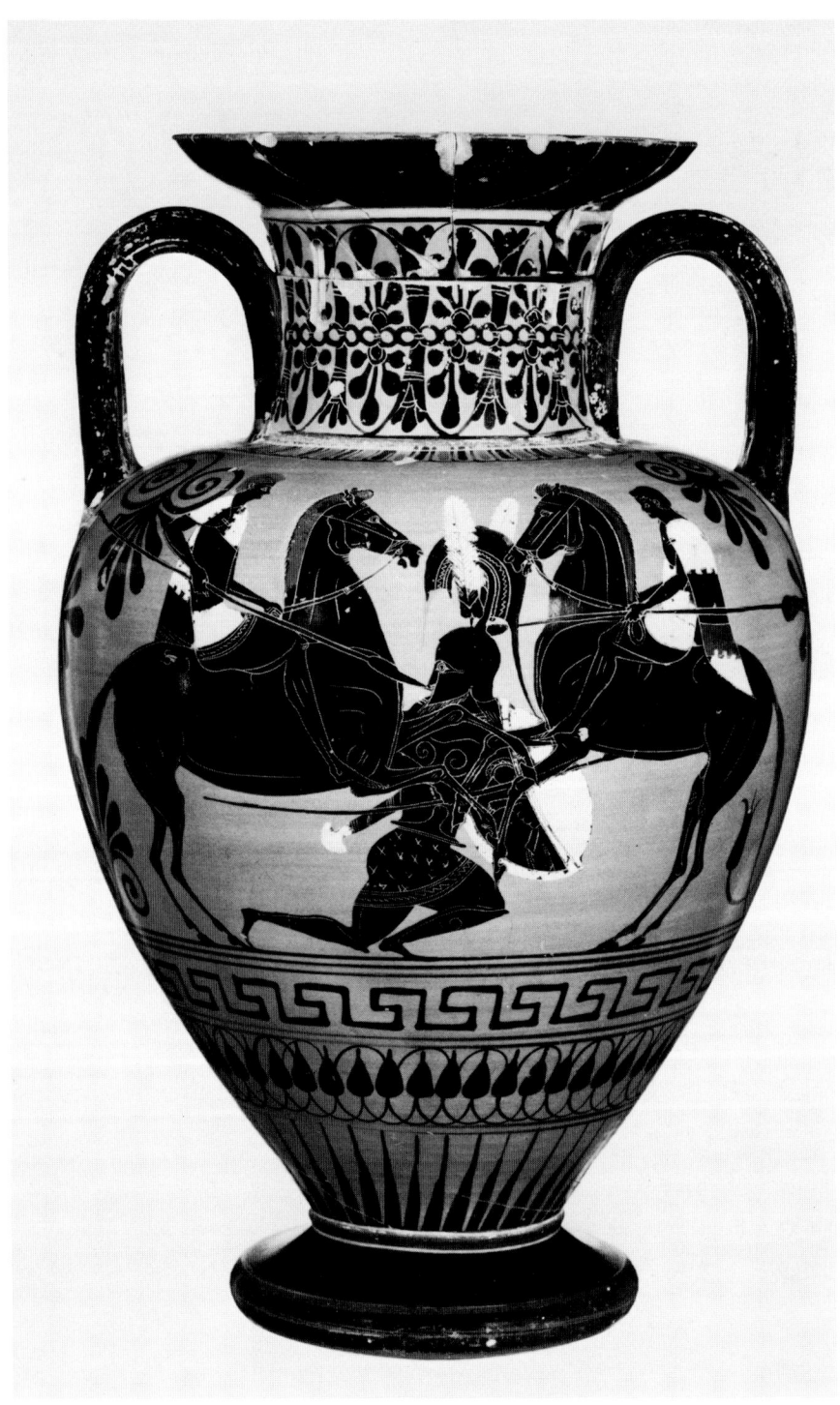

**10. Neck Amphora
Attributed to the Medea Group,
Bareiss Painter (name piece)
Circa 520-510 B.C.
Height: 33 cm.
Checklist no. 47.**

This is a standard amphora shape from the penultimate decade of the sixth century. The obverse represents Herakles standing behind a quadriga with Athena as charioteer. She is about to drive the hero to Olympos where he will be received by the gods as one of them. On the reverse, two riders fight with spears over a fallen hoplite. The subjects belong to the standard repertory of late black-figure; the drawing is good without being a masterpiece. However, two features distinguish the amphora. First, it is the name piece of an artist known from several other vases, thus contributing to a better understanding of this phase of Attic vase painting. Second, and more importantly, the vase was repaired in antiquity with the upper neck and mouth of another amphora of the same dimensions. The two parts were joined by bronze wire set in specially carved grooves. The substitute mouth comes from a vase made at least a decade more recently; thus the original amphora must have been in use for some time before it happened to break. Vases mended in antiquity have survived in reasonable numbers, but repairs made with alien pieces are rather rare. The widespread opinion is that repairs prove that Greek vases were precious objects, not for everyday use; however, the repairs also may demonstrate that ceramics were mended for purely utilitarian reasons.

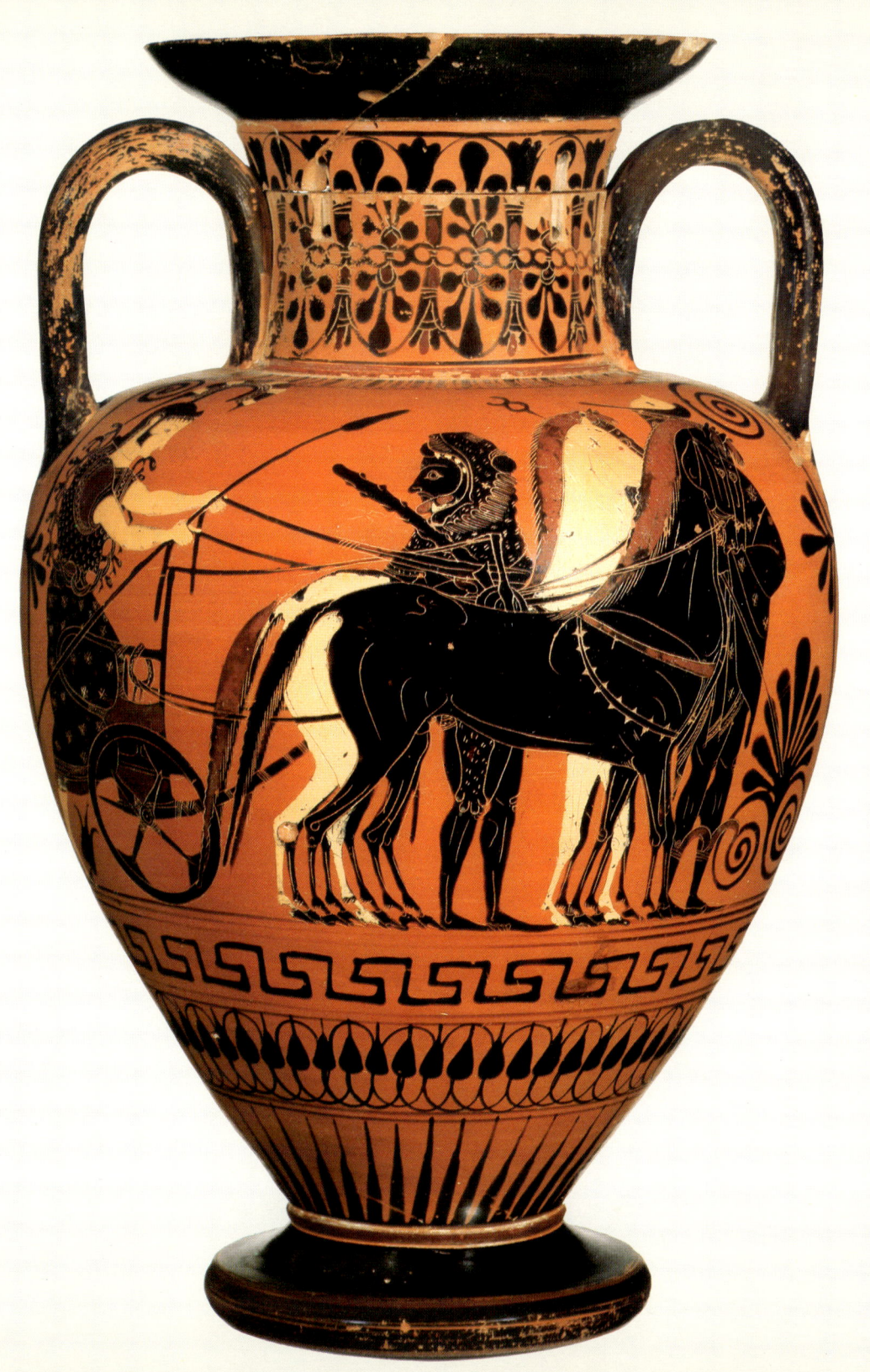

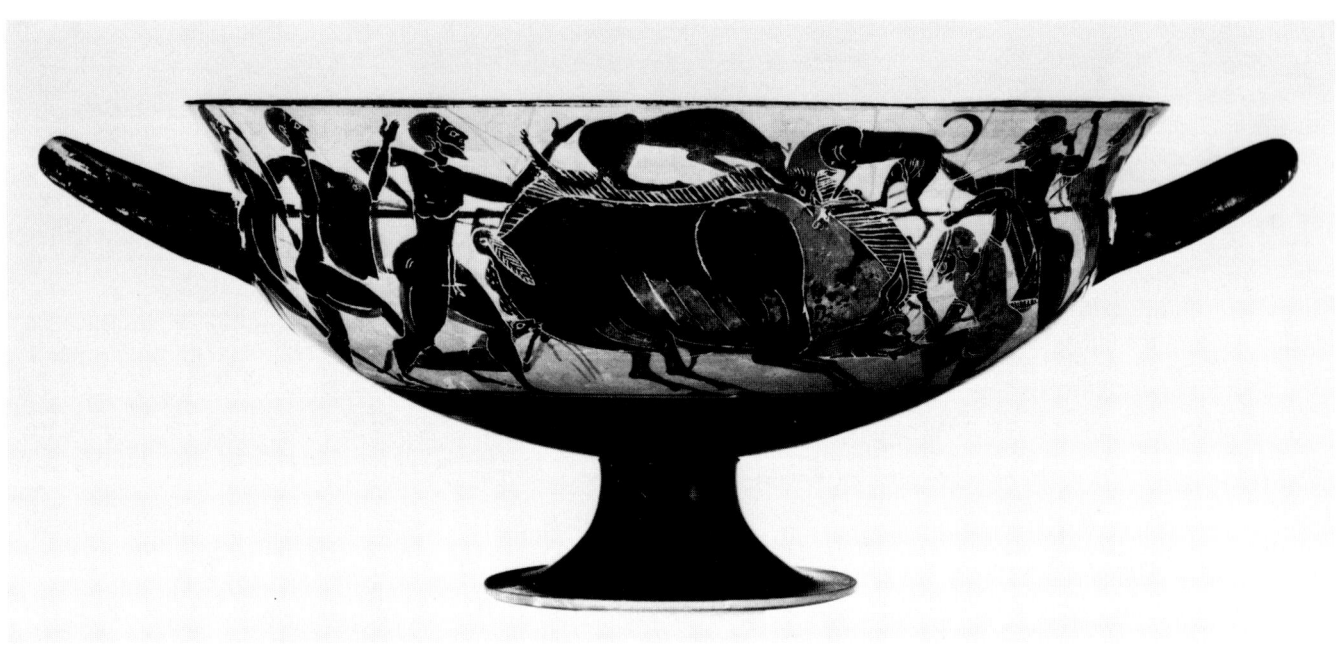
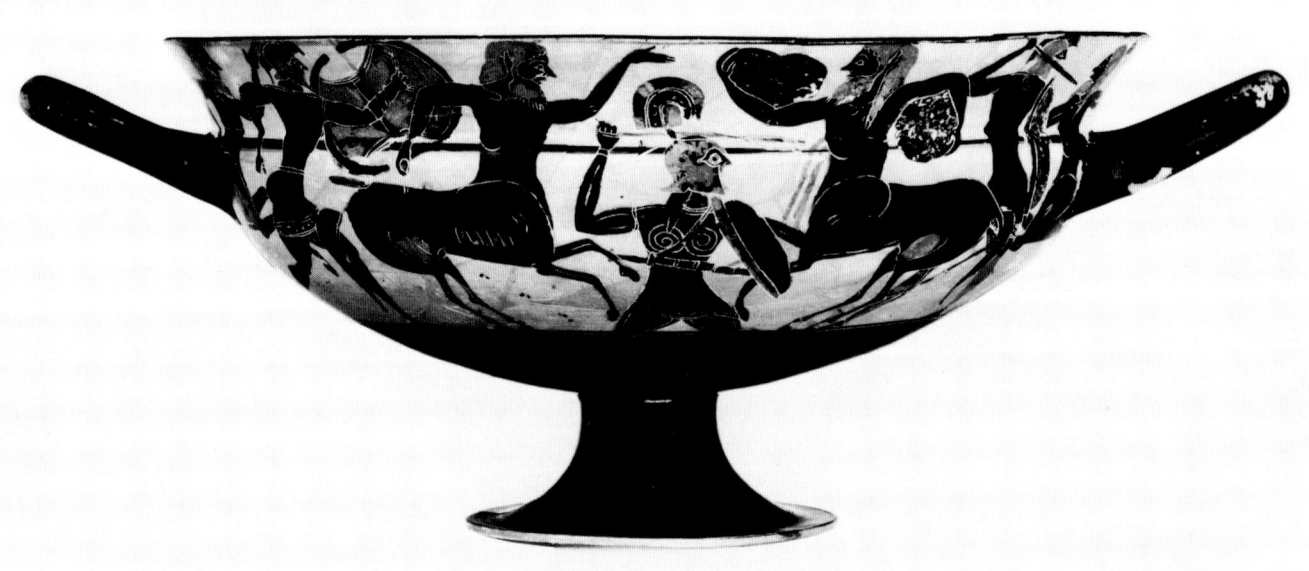

11. Siana Cup (Overlap Decoration)
Circa 580-570 B.C.
Height: 12.9 cm.
Diameter: 26.2 cm.
Checklist no. 83.

The clearly articulated exterior of the Siana cup presents two possibilities for decoration: either the bowl and lip can be treated as two separate zones or they can be considered one single ground for the figures. The latter is the choice here, and this scheme of decoration is called "overlap." On side A is the mythical Calydonian boar hunt, with six men and three dogs actively attacking the huge animal who was sent by Artemis to ravage Calydon. Side B has a scene from the battle between the centaurs and the Lapiths. The half-horse, half-human centaurs provoked the battle by trying to carry off the women at the wedding of the Lapith king Perithoos. Here, in the center of the scene, the Lapith hero Kaineus is being beaten into the ground with stones, the only way in which he could be destroyed.

Except for a reserved tondo and a reserved line around the inside rim, the interior of a Siana cup is black. The tondo is conventionally decorated with a figural composition, here a mounted rider to right, and framed with tongues, alternately red and black with white dots in the interstices, which are set between two groups of concentric circles.

The Siana cup takes its name from a cemetery on Rhodes where two examples of the shape were found. It is an early black-figure vase type which slowly disappeared as the Little Master cups became popular (see Nos. 12 and 13). The profile is standardized, with a wide lip sharply offset from the deep bowl which bulges out beneath it; a low, flaring foot; and handles at the sides attached just beneath the lip. The decoration is elaborate, though somewhat more variable from one example to another than is the vase shape.

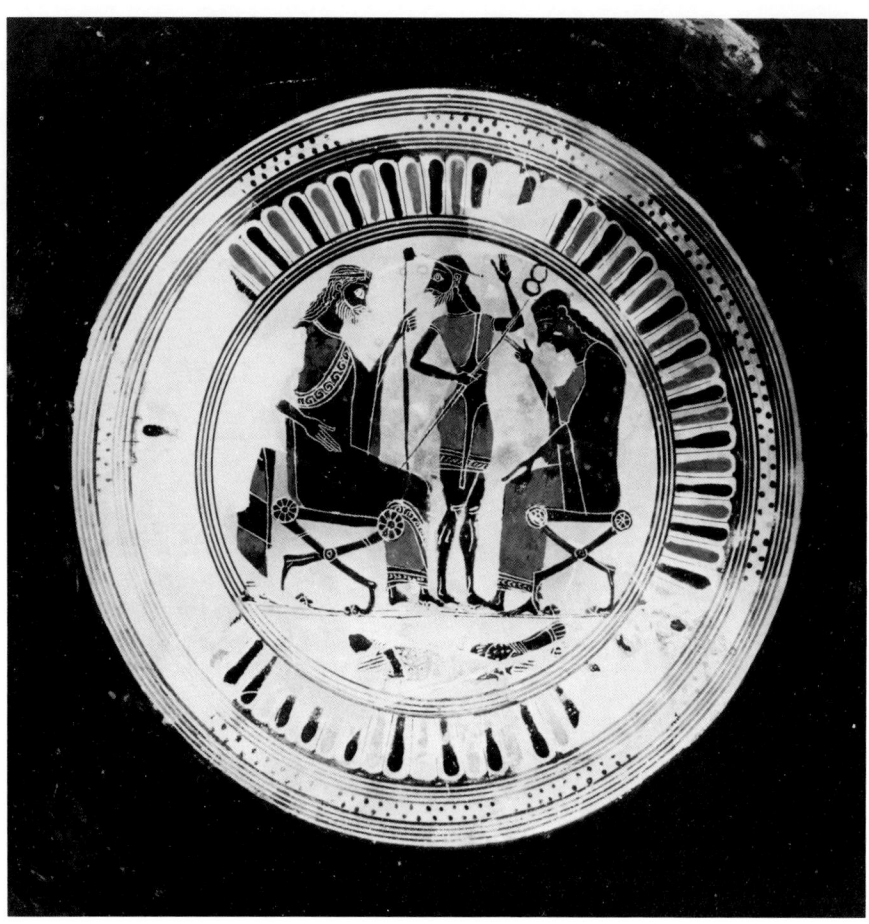

12. Lip Cup
Signed by Epitimos the potter
Circa 550-540 B.C.
Height: restored
Diameter: 30.5 cm.
Checklist no. 86.

13. Lip Cup
Attributed to the Tleson Painter
Circa 540 B.C.
Height: 11.5 cm.
Diameter: 19.8 cm.
Checklist no. 88.

Lip cups are one type of a class called "Little Master" cups. Their popularity in antiquity is attested by the large number which have survived. They are named for the most obvious feature of their profile, the lip which is clearly offset from the bowl; but the entire profile and the scheme of decoration are fairly well standardized. The bowl is rather deep, completely black inside except for the reserved tondo and a reserved line inside the rim. Outside, the lip and handle zone are reserved, though divided by a black line which marks the offset; the lower bowl is black with a reserved line about halfway between the lower border of the handle zone and the top of the stem. The stem and top of the foot are black; the outer edge of the footplate is reserved. The handles are painted outside, reserved within. However, as the two examples here clearly demonstrate, size was a variable.

The smaller cup (No. 13), is a perfect example of the shape. A fighting cock, done in the miniaturistic style that distinguishes the Little Masters, is centered on the lip on either side. The painting has been attributed to the Tleson Painter. Named for the well-known potter Tleson, whose signed cups he invariably decorated, he may be Tleson himself. Light, simple, and elegant, the cup is as pleasing to the hand as it is to the eye.

The larger cup (No. 12) is far more elaborate. It is signed outside across both handle zones: ΕΠΙΤΙΜΟΣ ΕΠΟΙ]ΕΣΕ[Ν ("Epitimos made me"). Inside, within a broad circular frame of alternating red and black tongues, concentric circles, and a dotted band, are four Olympians. Zeus sits to the right on a folding stool, scepter in hand, facing Hera, who is also seated. Between them, Hermes stands to the right with his *kerykeion*. Leaving to deliver a message, he looks back toward the figure who stands behind Zeus. Only a bit of drapery survives, but this may be Hebe, the cupbearer of the gods. The composition, enlivened with added red and white paint, is set on a simple groundline. In the exergue below are confronted cocks. The lip is decorated on each side of the exterior with a rider facing right. Rampant sphinxes stand with front paws resting on the handle roots, their bodies facing the handles and their heads turned back toward the potter's signatures.

The cup was burned in antiquity, so that its natural reddish color has been altered and some of the details obscured. But, in spite of the damage, it is still an imposing example of both the potter's craft and the vase painter's art.

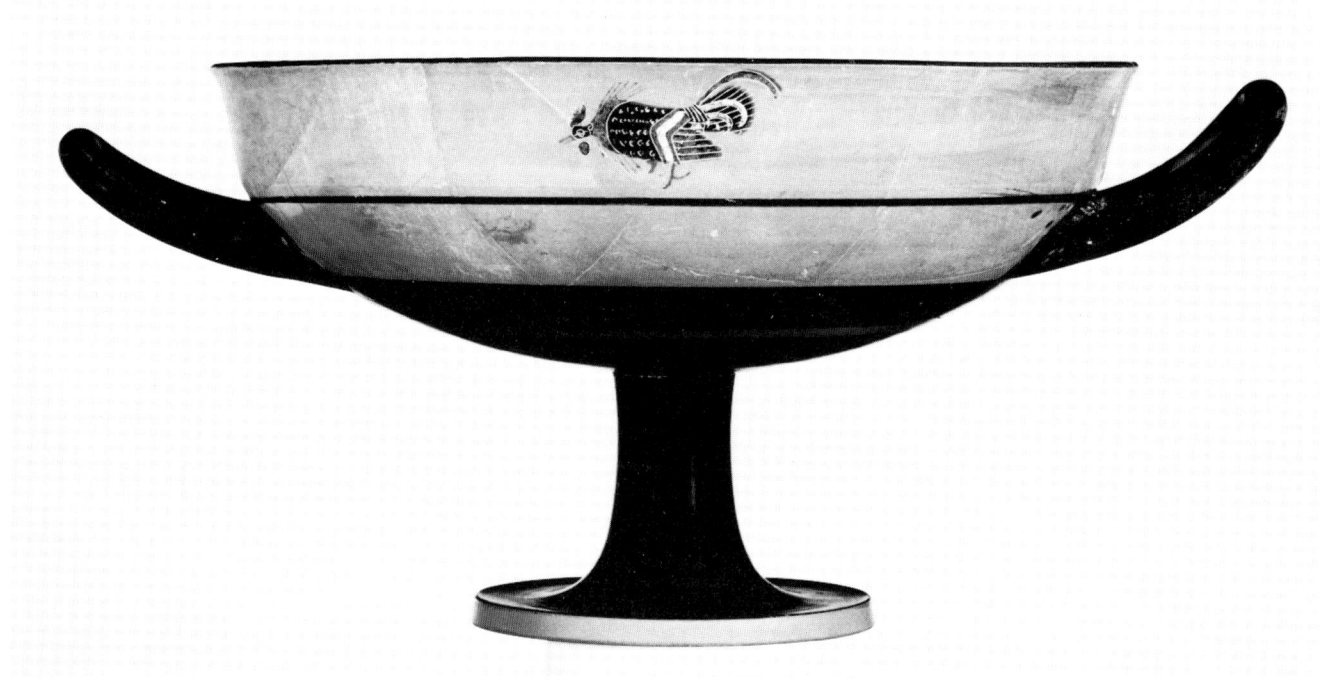

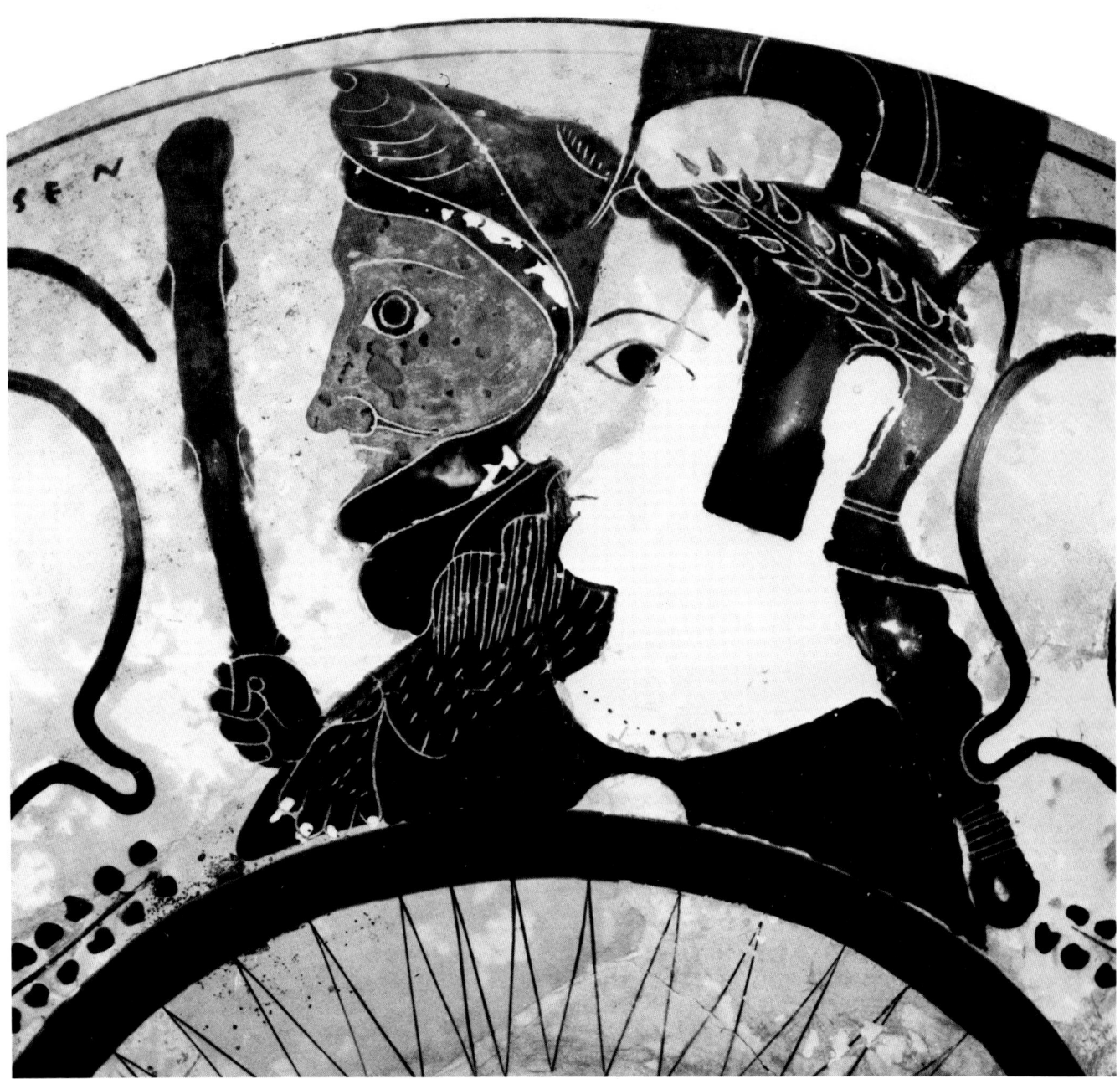

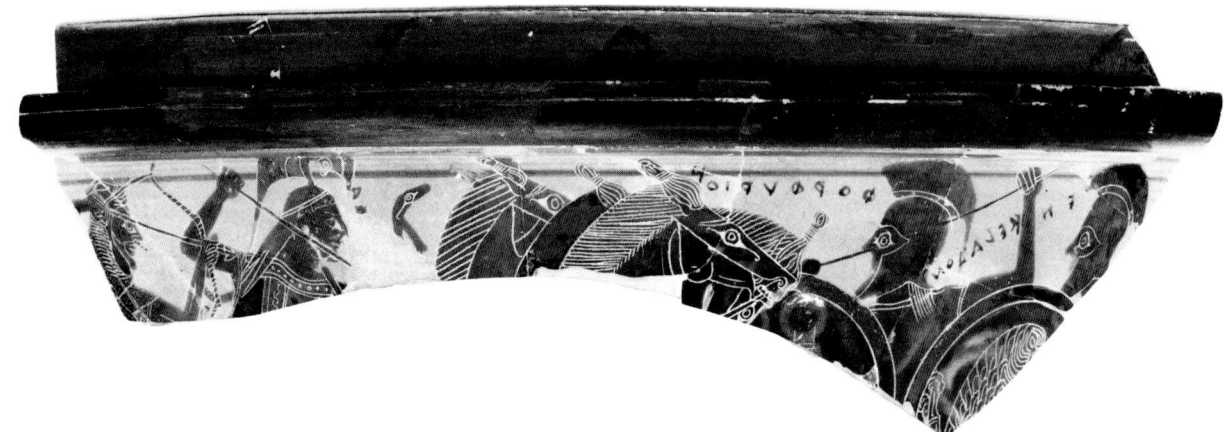

14. Cup Type A
Signed by Nikosthenes as potter
Circa 530 B.C.
Height: 11.4 cm.
Diameter: 27.2 cm.
Checklist no. 94.

15. Pyxis Fragment
Attributed to the BMN Painter
Circa 540 B.C.
Height: 6.8 cm.
Original diameter (est.): 22.2 cm.
Checklist no. 75.

Nikosthenes has left us more signatures than any other Attic potter. He manifestly liked to see his name written, and he also liked new fashions—his very active workshop was one of the first to adopt the new red-figure technique and many other innovations. But his taste was not always the best. Most of his signatures survive on the countless Nicosthenic amphorae, surely not the most elegant of the vase shapes of the time (fragments of two Nicosthenic amphorae are included in the exhibition, Checklist nos. 49 and 50). Nikosthenes may have invented the emphatic shape for the export market in Etruria, but little excuse can be found for the quality of the painted decoration found on these amphorae. The same hands painted other shapes as well, but fortunately some competent craftsmen also worked in Nikosthenes' workshop, among them the excellent painter Lydos (for his work, see above No. 5).

One of them painted this signed cup. The potter has thrown a deep, well-proportioned vessel, designed to enhance the pleasure of a good drink. The decoration is pleasant and attractive. Busts of divinities take the place of the nose one would expect between two apotropaic eyes (cf. No. 3 above). On one side Hades, the king of the Underworld, appears beside Demeter, his unwilling mother-in-law, and Persephone, whom he abducted. Close to the potter's signature on the other side is Herakles with his protectress Athena. The groupings are significant, but the main intention of the painter was the creation of an attractive and effective decoration enhanced by extensive use of added red and white and by the figures of animals (a rooster and a boar) under the handles.

Another product of Nikosthenes' workshop reproduced here is a fragment of a shape which modern archaeologists call the Nicosthenic pyxis, as it is probable that he invented it. A deep bowl, with the rim offset to allow for the lid and a solid foot, presents a large surface for decoration, and the painter used it here for a continuous representation of the battle of the gods and giants. Herakles and Athena fight close together, the hero on foot, the goddess from her chariot. Their adversaries' names are inscribed: Enkelados is the usual opponent of Athena, while Porphyrion (the painter must have pronounced the first letter with marked aspiration, as he misspelled it as Phorphyrion) often fights with Zeus. The artist of the drawing is called the BMN Painter—short for British Museum Nikosthenes, after a piece in that museum. He decorated another vase in the Bareiss Collection—a Siana cup with the Calydonian boar hunt (see Checklist no. 85). The BMN painter was a solid craftsman without great artistic pretension, but he must have been the best painter steadily employed by Nikosthenes.

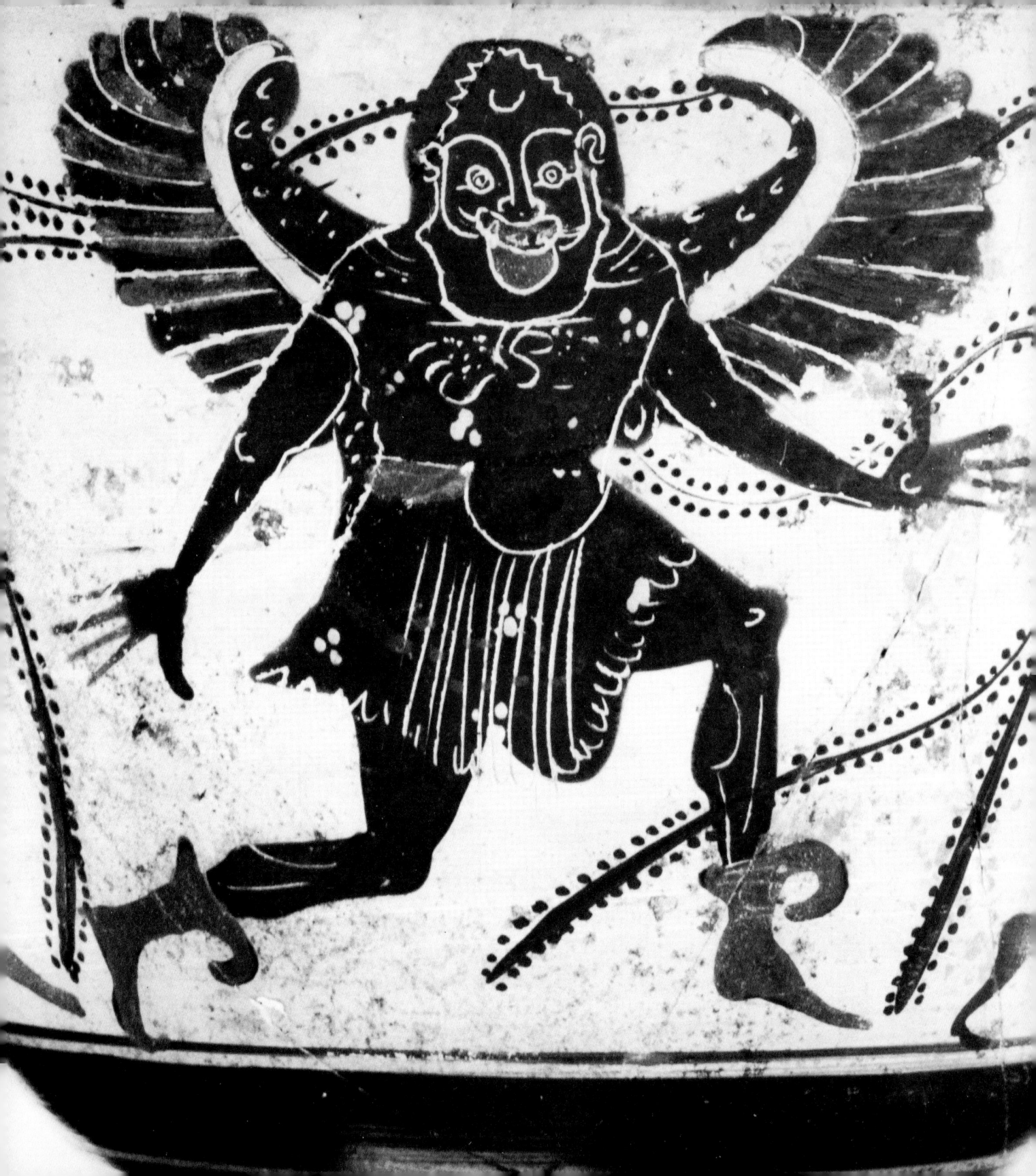

16. White-ground Kyathos
Attributed to a follower of the Theseus Painter
Circa 510 B.C.
Height with handle: 14.8 cm.
Diameter: 11 cm.
Checklist no. 79.

The kyathos, or one-handled dipper, is a shape borrowed by the Greeks from the Etruscans and perhaps made exclusively for the Etruscan market. Its metallic prototype is echoed in the sharp profile of the vase; in the elegant high handle with the relief decoration at the top and along the inner face; in the remarkably thin, flaring walls of the cup; and in the curves of the foot. Evidence suggests that the workshop of the potter Nikosthenes was responsible for the introduction of the shape (see Nos. 14 and 15).

This same innovative workshop was also one of the earliest to employ the white-ground technique which is used here so effectively. Instead of setting the black figures against the natural orange-red color of the clay fabric, the artist has chosen to cover the vase with a fine white slip which offers greater contrast. Upon this, he has set an unusual scene of Perseus pursuing the three Gorgon sisters. Perseus, the son of Zeus and Danaë, was sent to take the head of the Gorgon Medusa. He did this with Athena's assistance, but he was afterwards pursued by Medusa's two remaining sisters. The more common representation shows Perseus being chased by the two immortal sisters. The black-figure technique depended upon incision to define the inner details. This cup is an exquisite example of the attention lavished on even a minor vase shape. Added red

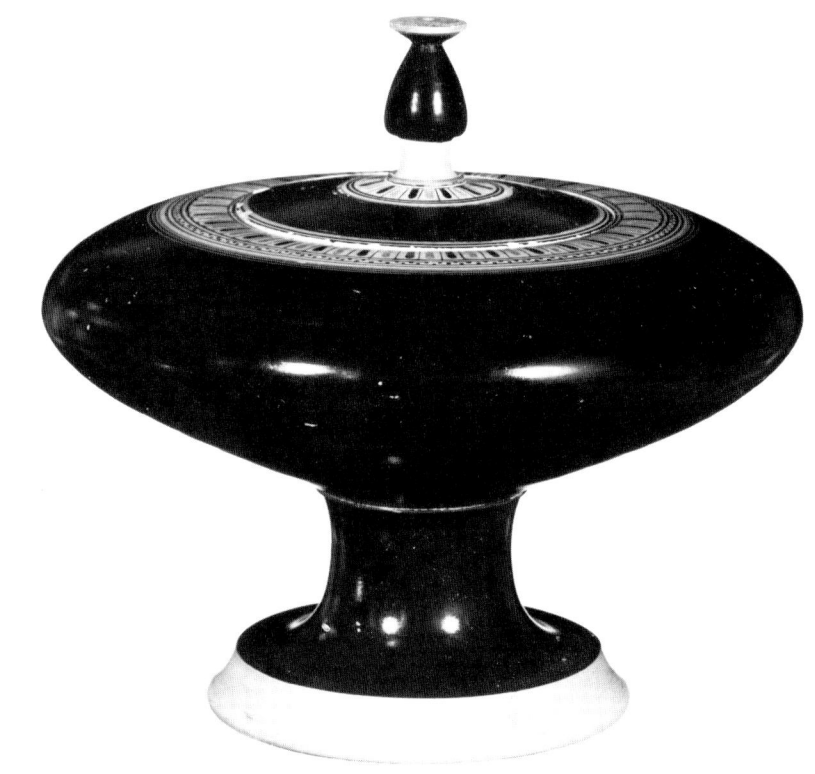

and white markings on the black forms further enhance the decorative effect, and the four figures are executed with the care of a miniaturist.

17. Exaleiptron
Circa 500 B.C.
Height (with lid): 15.5 cm.
Checklist no. 96.

A simple black vase with minimal ornamental decoration provides a real opportunity for appreciation of the potters' craft. The throwing is as perfect as the glaze. The excellent proportions contrast with the tense contour of the shape. The internal part of the vessel includes the solid foot, which turns into a wide body. The simple lid has a knob handle shaped like an exclamation point. The external elegance conceals some serious functional limitations: the sunken rebord of the body makes pouring out the whole contents—powder or liquid—almost impossible.

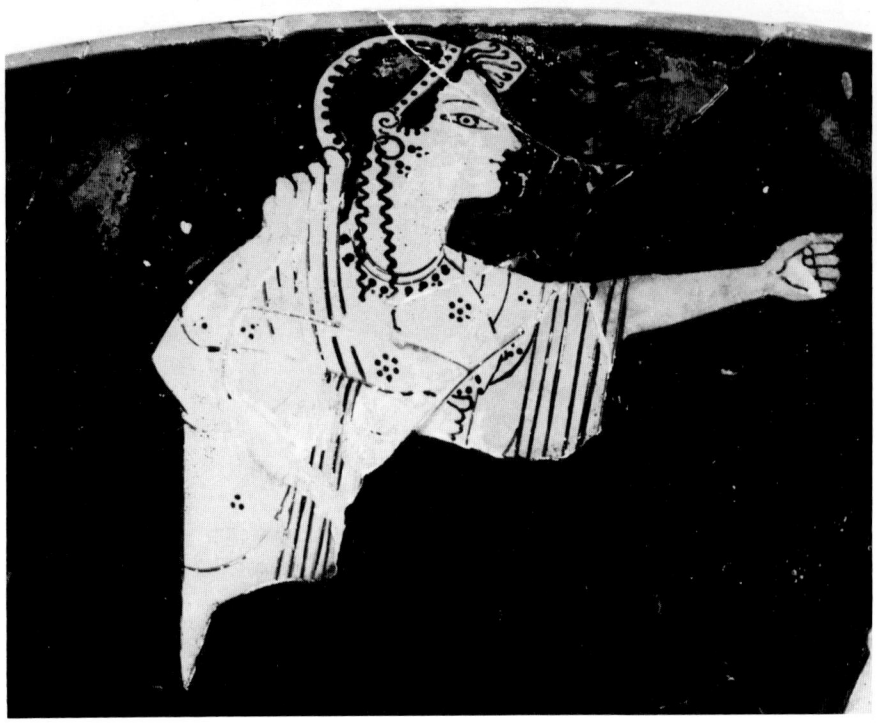

18. Cup Type A
Attributed to Psiax
Circa 520 B.C.
Height (as restored): 11 cm.
Diameter: 27.4 cm.
Checklist no. 142.

Psiax is one of a group of Attic vase painters who worked equally well in both black- and red-figure techniques. Recent research indicates that he may have been trained as a red-figure artist in the workshop of Andokides, the innovator of the new style, and simply chose to work in both techniques during this transitional period. This vase, badly burned in antiquity and since refired, is executed entirely in red-figure. The clay has lost its warm red color, and the black surfaces have been extensively harmed by exposure to fire. But even in this damaged state, the fragments which survive give some indication of the superb quality of the original vase. Many of the decorative details betray the artist's sympathies with the black-figure technique.

In the tondo, a simple reserved circle surrounds a pair of male figures. The right man has his arm around the shoulder of his youthful companion, who holds his left hand up toward his friend as if offering a flower. The himation of the left figure is decorated with dot rosettes; and, like the mantle of the right figure, it falls in rather brittle folds. Bothmer has pointed out that the appearance of the groundline within the tondo here is the earliest occurrence of this feature on a red-figure cup.

Outside, figures of men, youths, and women are arranged, mostly in pairs. There is surely music (one figure holds a lyre and another plays the double flutes, the pipes added in white) and wine (one hand offers a white kylix). But this is an elegant tableau, not a bawdy revel. The patterns on the drapery, the strands of hair, and the delicate features of the faces, which would have been indicated with incision or added color in black-figure, are drawn in fine relief lines with the same exquisite care and sense of decorative patterning as the palmette-lotus border in black silhouette that runs beneath the party.

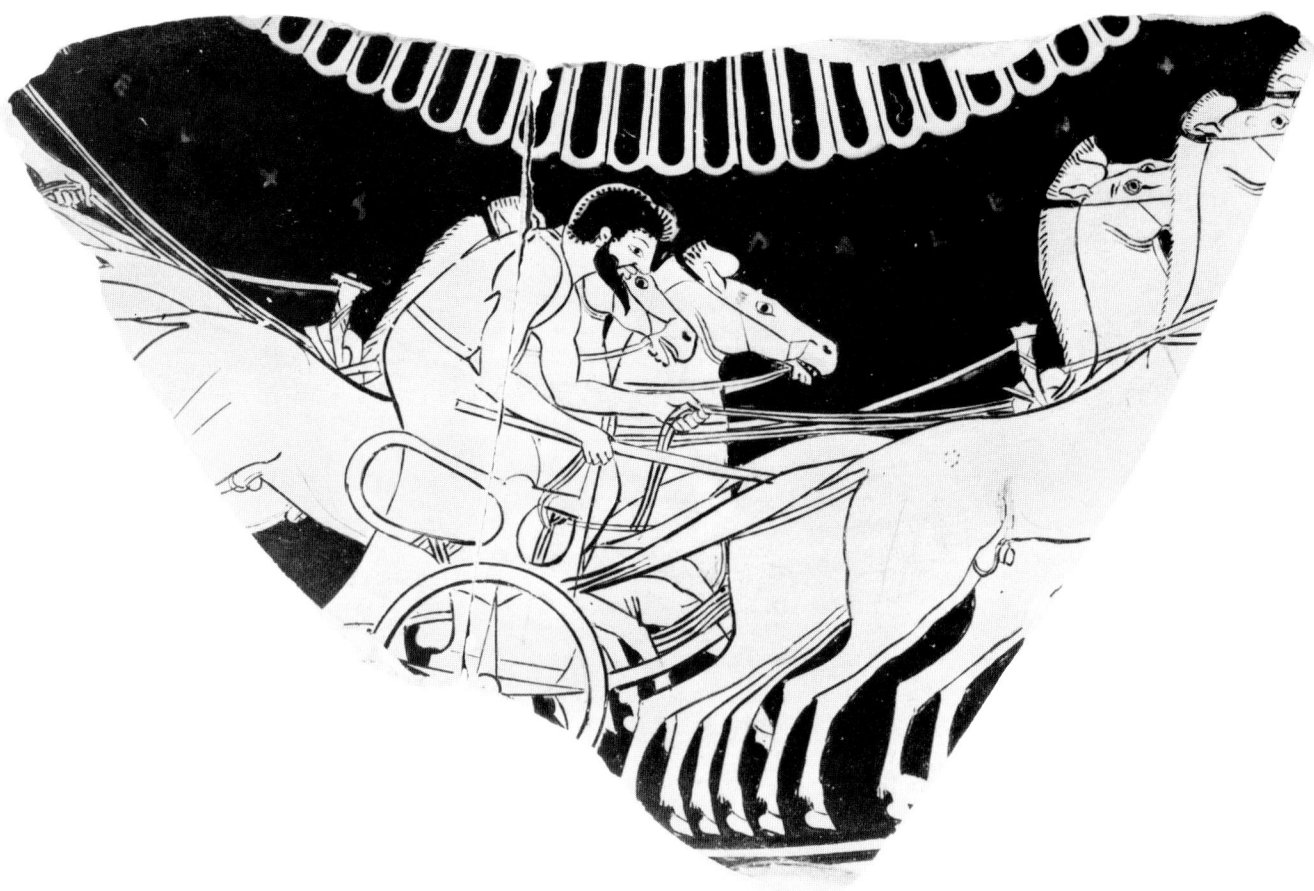

19. Hydria Fragment
Attributed to the Pioneer Group
Circa 520 B.C.
Height: 14.6 cm.
Checklist no. 111.

This handsome fragment from a red-figure hydria is a perfect example of the fact that not all Greek vases can be attributed to a definite painter. The piece was placed by Beazley in association with the Pioneers, the great masters of the second generation of red-figure vase painting, but without being designated specifically as the work of Euphronios or Euthymides or Phintias. Even without a great name attached, the drawing is excellent.

Only a part of the shoulder survives, depicting a scene of a quadriga race. A team of four thoroughbred horses—one of them with a brand on his hindquarters—is reined in by the charioteer, probably because it is racing too fast into a curve, while another quadriga tries to pass at full speed. The most prized victory at any of the panhellenic games—for example the quadrennial games at Olympia—was in the chariot race. The rich owner of the stable was credited with the success, not the charioteer; but the victory of the horses depended on the charioteer's discipline and skill, and this point is well captured in this drawing.

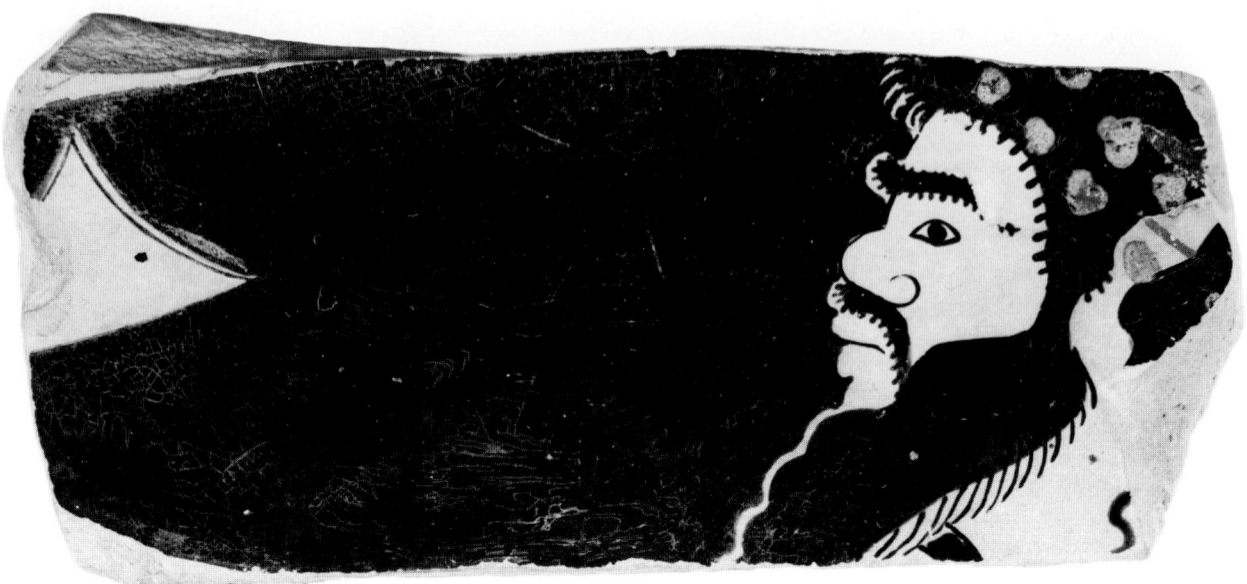

**20. Calyx Krater Fragment
Attributed to Smikros
Circa 520 B.C.
Width: 8.6 cm.
Checklist no. 105.**

Little remains of a large red-figure calyx krater except the head of a satyr and part of the drinking horn he is holding. But the quality of the drawing remains striking. The skillful rendering of the hirsute eyebrow and beard and the grimacing expression of the wild man are rather superior to the usually modest products of Smikros, who was Euphronios' pupil and faithful companion. One is tempted to believe that the master retouched this drawing, as he did perhaps some of the other, better products of Smikros; it may even be possible that Euphronios allowed Smikros to sign Euphronios' own drawings, as, for example, the recently acquired amphora in Berlin.

**21. Neck Amphora
Attributed to the Berlin Painter
Circa 480 B.C.
Height: 30.5 cm.
Checklist no. 97.**

**22. Kalpis Fragment
Attributed to the Berlin Painter
Circa 480-470 B.C.
Height (approx.): 20.5 cm.
Width: 33 cm.
Checklist no. 114.**

In the early fifth century, there was a pleiad of outstanding artists among the Attic red-figure vase painters. They can be divided into two main groups according to the vase shapes which they preferred to decorate. As the Athenians seemed to enjoy good wine more than ever, production of cups increased considerably, enhanced still more because the Etruscans developed a taste for this shape. Consequently, many vase painters specialized in decorating cups, including such excellent artists as Onesimos, the Brygos Painter and his circle, Makron, and Douris, all well represented in the Bareiss Collection. Others, less numerous but not less distinguished, preferred to paint pots, perhaps because the larger surfaces offered a better opportunity for monumental creations. The names of the two best pot painters remain unknown; one is called the Kleophrades Painter after a potter in whose atelier he worked for a while, the other is the Berlin Painter, whose name amphora is in a museum in that city.

Two vases in the Bareiss Collection represent two phases of the Berlin Painter's art: the neck amphora (No. 21) is earlier, about 480 B.C.; the fragment of a kalpis (No. 22) is later, after 480 B.C. The amphora's distinctive shape is thrown with a precision and taste for proportion which are characteristic of the Berlin Painter's drawing. Perhaps he was both potter and painter. With a minimum of subsidiary decoration, he placed a single figure on each side of the vase. On the front is a young reveler holding a cup, which he has probably used abundantly, as reflected in his dance-like stance. But, in comparison with the jolly revelers of other painters, this youth appears rather serious; and one is induced to believe that the complicated pose results more from the artistic intention of the painter than from the effects of the wine. A strange man appears on the reverse: he is a barbarian servant, taking care of the young master. The painter registers the un-Greek features of the face with his usual clarity.

The kalpis features a scene of two figures, an armed Athena and a youth, leaving for a journey. Perhaps the painter had in mind the young Theseus under the auspices of the goddess. The unity of the shape and the representation is very marked, as there is no framing pattern. At the same time, the drawing is a little more relaxed than on the earlier vase of the Berlin Painter. Other artists may have liked wine, women, and song; the Berlin Painter loved the perfection of his art above all.

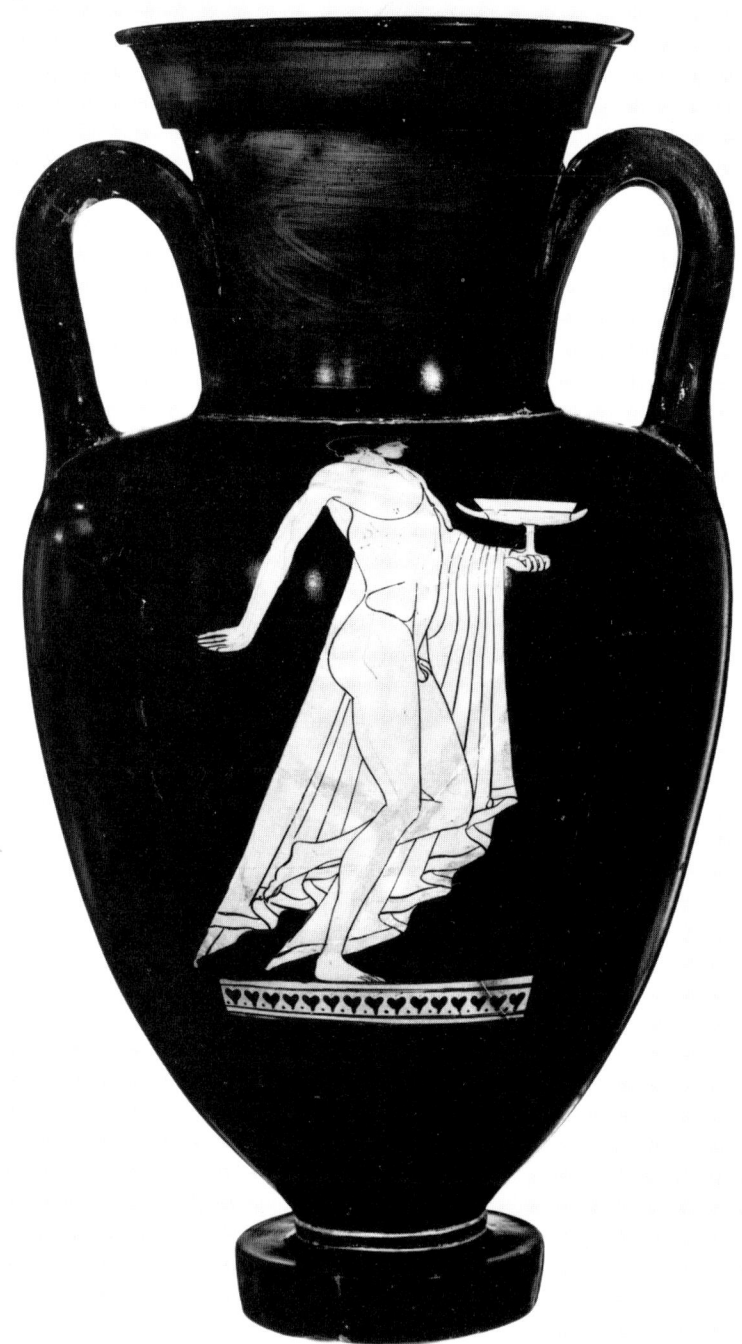

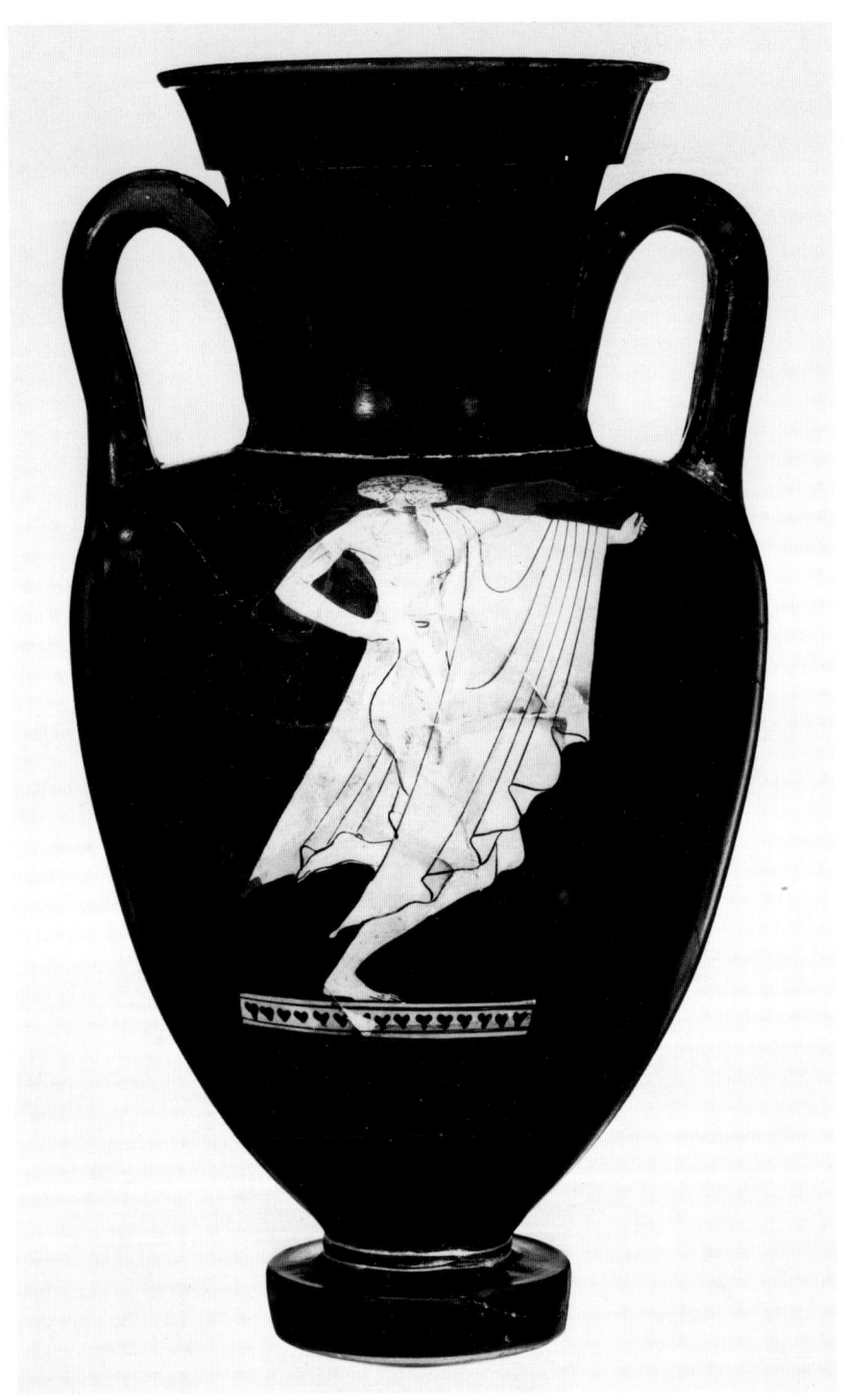

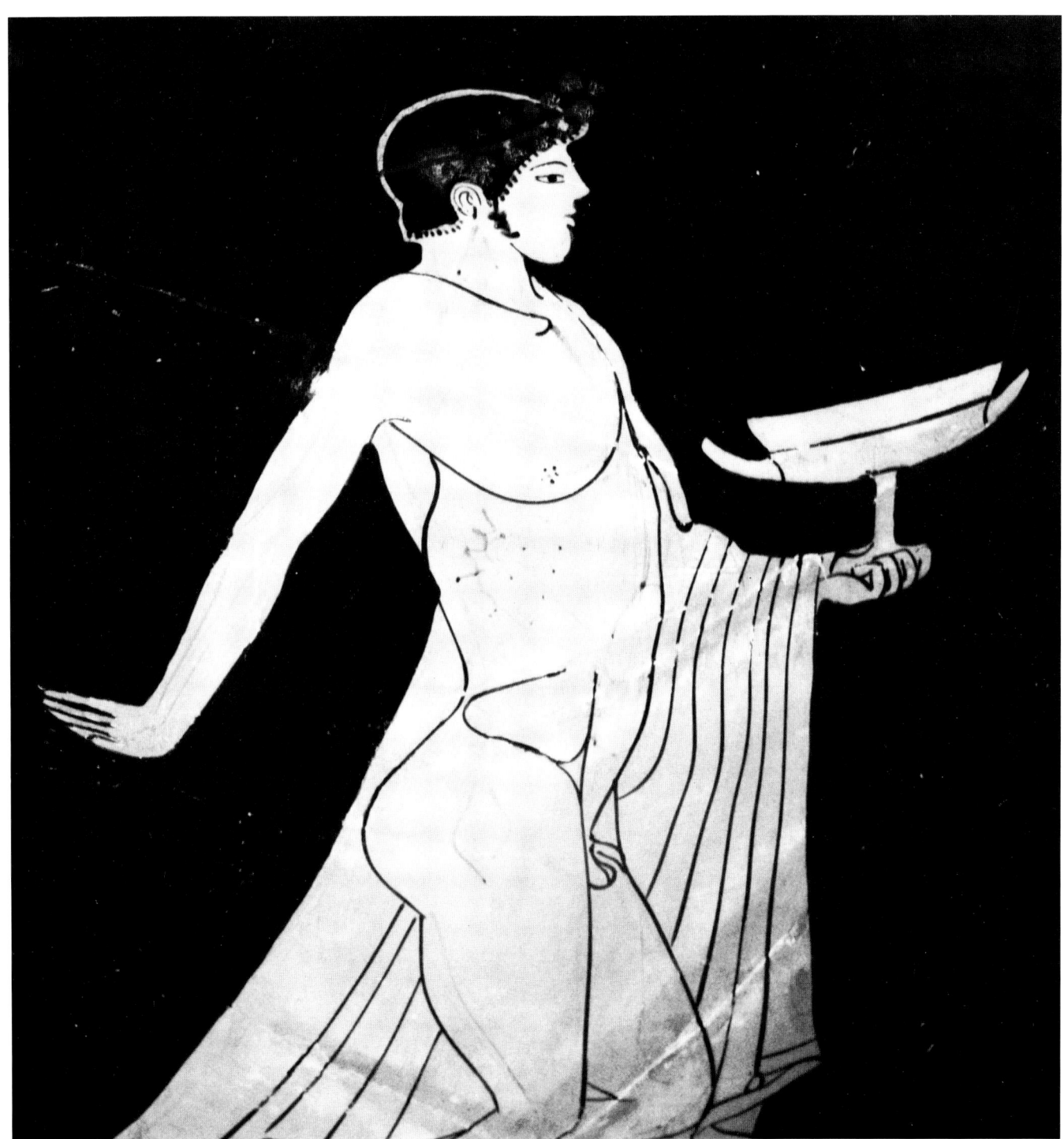

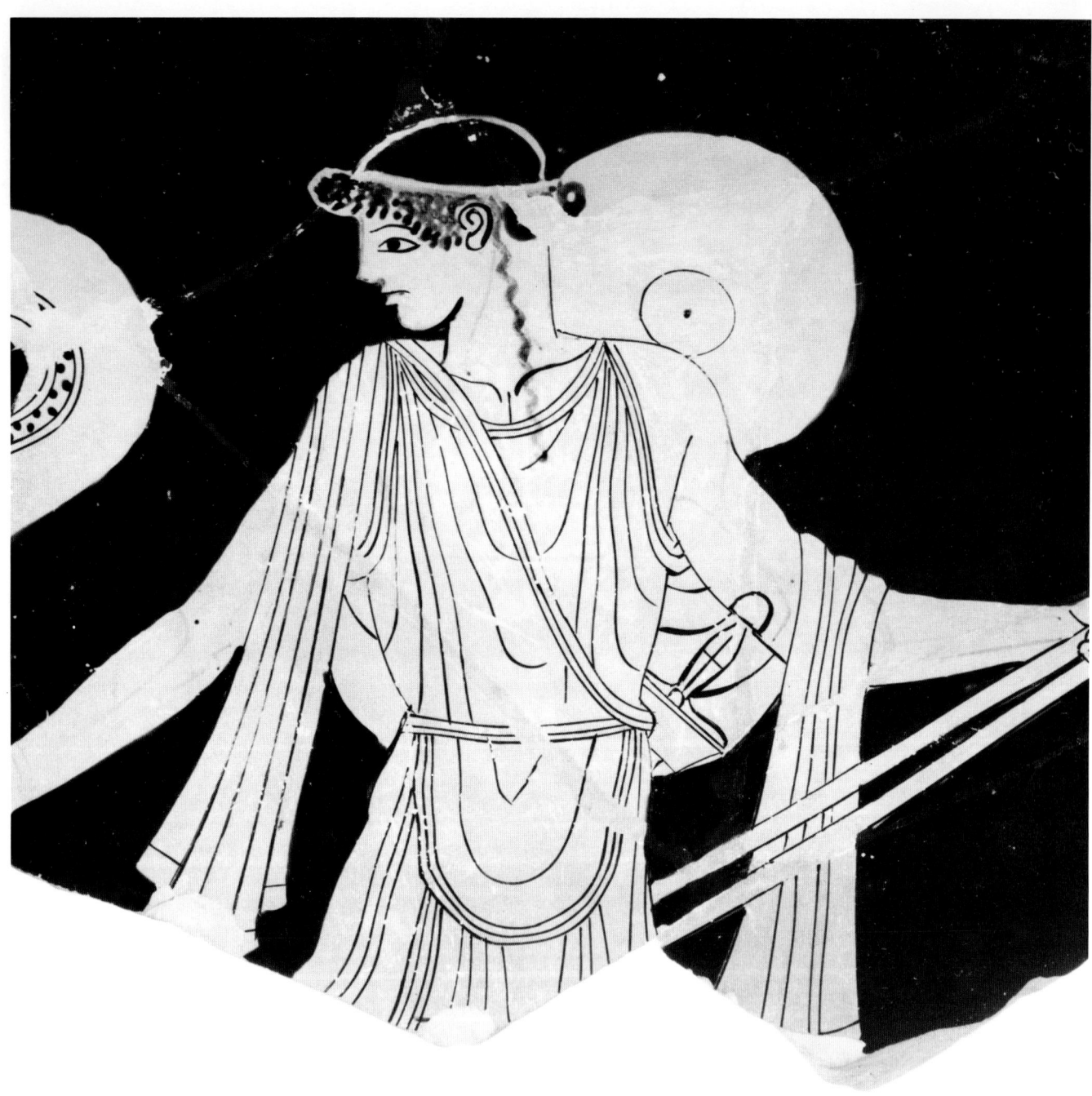

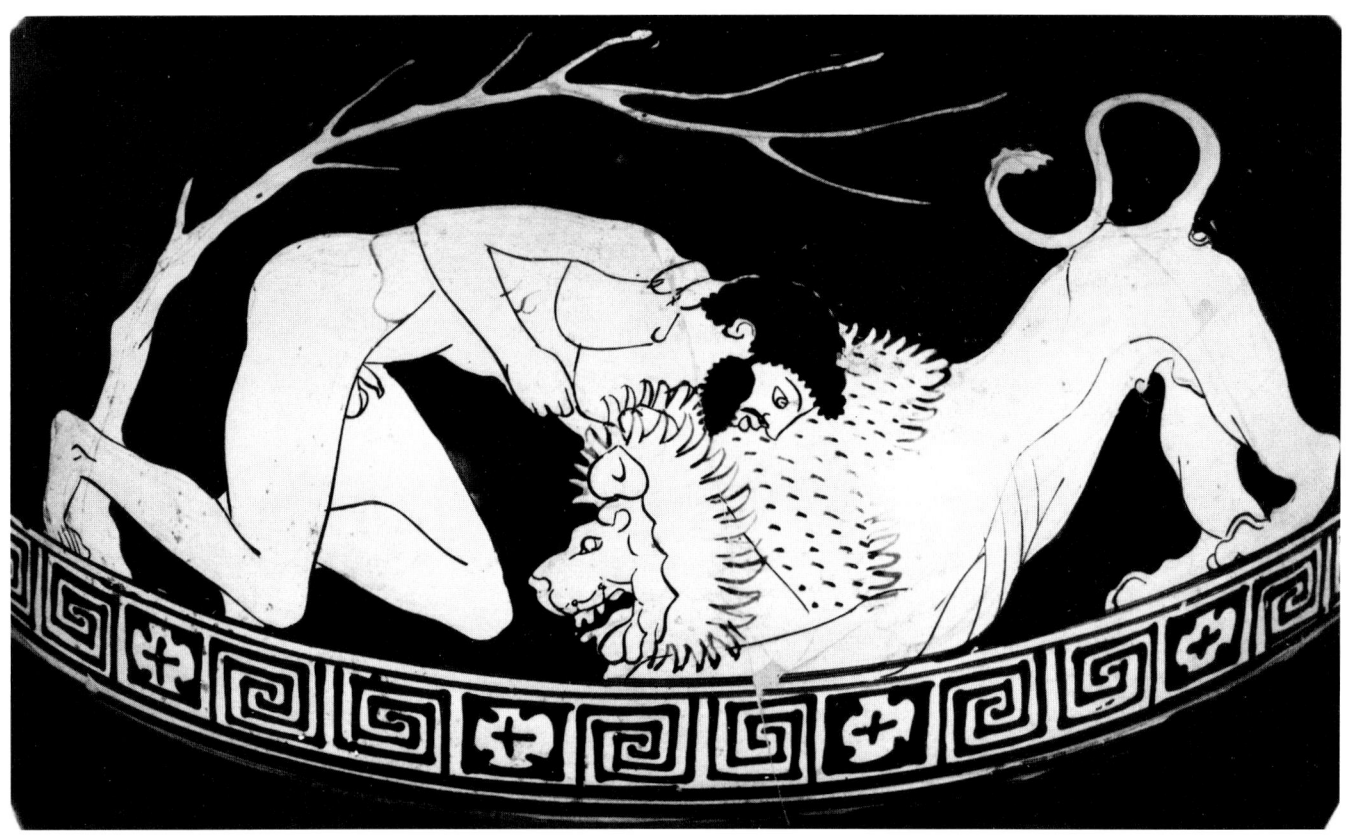

23. Kalpis
Attributed as probably by the Aegisthus Painter
Circa 470 B.C.
Height: 28 cm.
Checklist no. 116.

Herakles was indisputably the most popular hero in ancient Greece, and his struggle with the Nemean lion is the most frequently represented mythological subject in archaic vase painting. The painter who placed this scene on the shoulder of a kalpis about 470 B.C. was clearly inspired by previous models. His Herakles recalls the monumental figures of the Kleophrades Painter, while the lion has been reduced from a powerful beast to a creature of decorative, heraldic appearance. The painter has added a landscape element of his own: a tree is bent over the hero's back, completing the composition. The ground line is emphasized by a length of decorative maeander pattern. As usual, Herakles wins without any effort. The unbroken vase, with its brilliant glaze, is an outstanding example of the organic unity of shape and decoration.

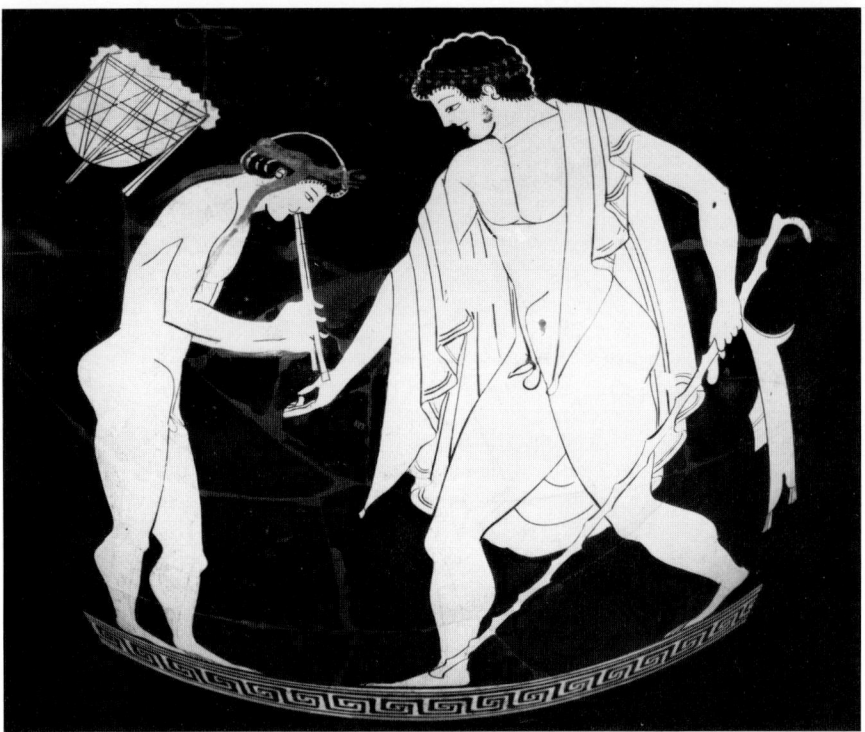

24. Kalpis
Attributed to the Eucharides Painter
Circa 480 B.C.
Height: 40 cm.
Checklist no. 112.

His cheeks puffed full of air, a boy plays the flute for a reveler who is just old enough to grow a downy beard. They must be about to leave a symposion—a provision basket hangs on the wall, the youth wears a wreath, and the boy sports a large red ribbon in his hair. The reveler holds the elegant walking stick appropriate to an Athenian dandy together with the flute case. He was surely a guest at the banquet, while the flutist provided paid entertainment during the evening pastime of the rich. Under the spell of wine and music, the youth approaches the boy with a gesture reminiscent of the courting scenes which begin to disappear at this time from the repertory of vase painting.

The Eucharides Painter is named after a beautiful boy he praised on his vases. ΚΑΛΟΣ ΕΥΧΑΡΙΔΕΣ—"Eucharides is beautiful"—is also written on this kalpis. Active in the first quarter of the fifth century, the Eucharides Painter was prolific both in the traditional black-figure and in the new red-figure. A solid craftsman, he was always ready to learn from the leading masters of his time: the drawing of this kalpis is clearly inspired by the Berlin Painter (see Nos. 21 and 22), especially the figure of the reveler.

25. Kalpis
Assigned to the Group of the Floral Nolans
Circa 480-470 B.C.
Height: 36 cm.
Checklist no. 115.

The owl was one of the symbols of Athena, patron goddess of the city of Athens. It had appeared alone on early coins of the city. In the last quarter of the sixth century B.C., it became the standard image on the reverse of Athenian silver issues, together with a branch of the olive tree, the goddess' gift to her city. These coins, with the profile of Athena on the obverse, became one of the most widely circulated currencies in the ancient world. Thus it is no surprise that the image on the curving shoulder of this Attic kalpis is related to the famous owl of the city's coinage. It stands here, as on the coins, with its body to the right and its head frontal. The artist has gone to great trouble to define each feather, carefully distinguishing the finer down of the breast from the longer, coarser quills on the edges of the wings. The single olive branch of the coins is now balanced by a second, and the two stand upright framing the bird, with one fruit attached to each.

The kalpis as a shape deserves special attention. It is a variant of the hydria, or water jug, introduced in the final quarter of the sixth century B.C. The standard black-figure hydria is more distinctly articulated, reflecting a metal prototype, with a wide horizontal mouth, short vertical neck, horizontal shoulder, and ovoid body (see also No. 9). Each of these clearly

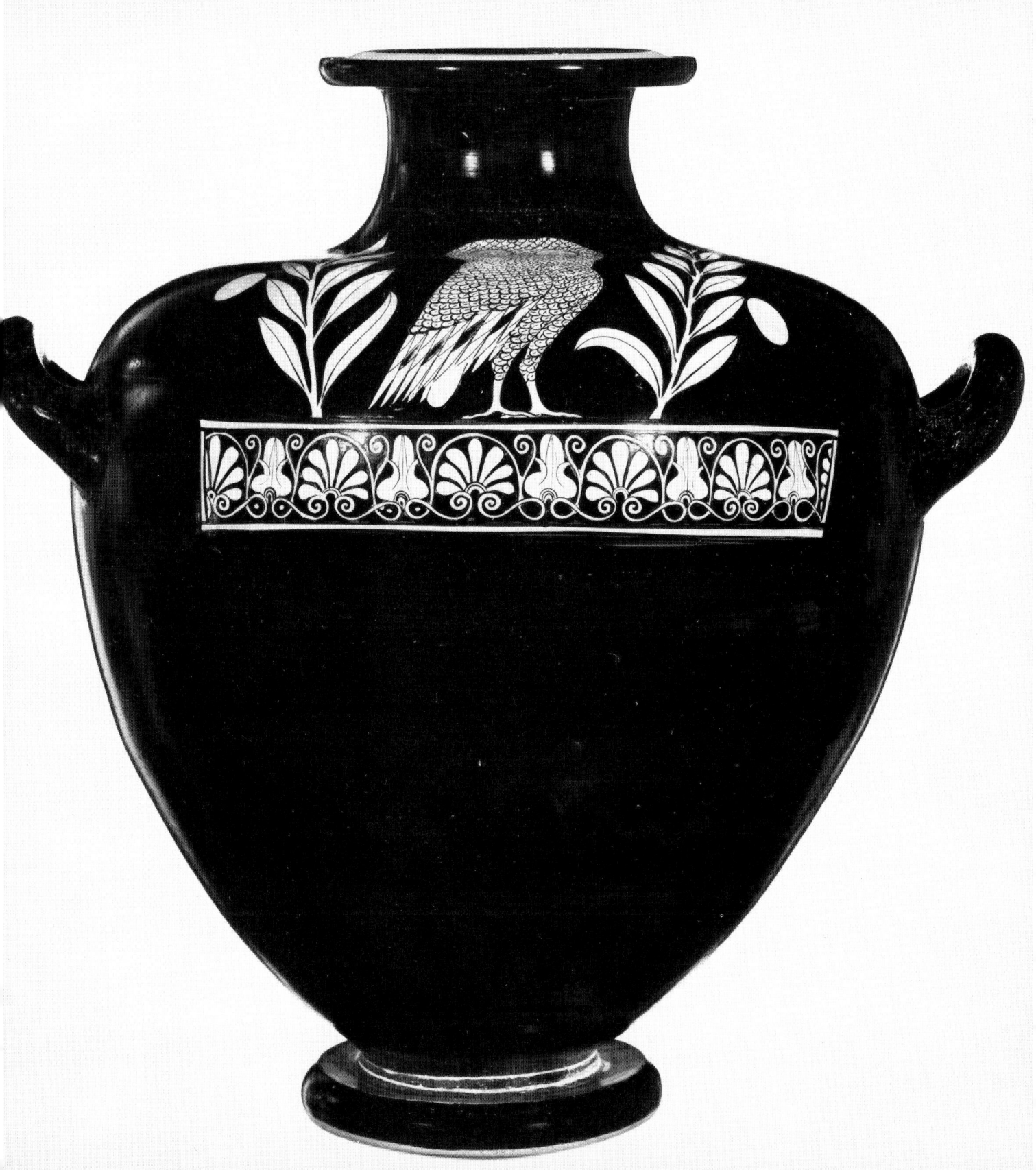

defined parts was made separately; and shoulder, neck, and body provided fields for painted decoration. The kalpis is, by contrast, a creation of the Attic potter. Neck, shoulder, and body are united by one continuous curving line, created in one piece on the potter's wheel. The Kalpis' vertical rear handle is much smaller in size than the standard hydria's and corresponds fairly closely in thickness to the side handles. Instead of separate zones for decoration, the vase painter now has only one irregular surface. This unity of curves and reverse curves was difficult to decorate. Late black- and early red-figure artists tried somewhat unsuccessfully to impose a rectangular panel on the shoulder as they had done on the earlier form. Later red-figure artists found a happier solution. Rather than avoid the awkward slope between shoulder and neck, they either accentuated it with an unframed composition (as here) or ignored it completely.

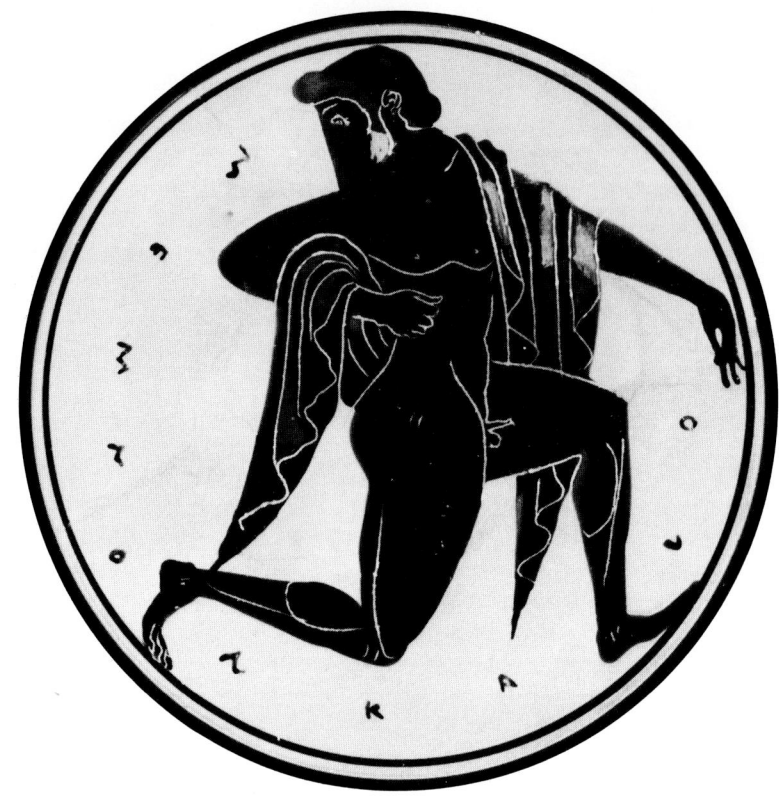

26. Cup Type A (Bilingual)
Attributed to Oltos
Potted by Hischylos
Circa 520 B.C.
Height: 13.1 cm.
Diameter: 32.5 cm.
Checklist no. 143.

27. Cup Type A
Attributed to Oltos
Potted by Hischylos
Circa 510 B.C.
Height: 13.2 cm.
Diameter: 33.1 cm.
Checklist no. 144.

Oltos began work as a vase painter in the last decades of the sixth century B.C., just after the time of transition from black- to red-figure. He is a red-figure artist, although he sometimes painted in the black-figure technique, for his black-figure compositions appear only on so-called "bilingual" vases, such as this eye cup (No. 26). Inside, in black-figure, a komast runs to the right, looking back over his shoulder. He wears a mantle striped with the same red which is used for his beard and the front of his hair. Details of body contours, musculature, and drapery folds are indicated by incision. Written in the field around him is MEMNON KAνO[S, an inscription that appears on nearly forty vases by Oltos. The exterior has palmettes at the handles, on side A, a youth, and on B, a nose between masculine eyes, all in red-figure.

Since a comparison of two similar figures is helpful to illustrate the difference in treatment from one technique to the other, we may look at the red-figure tondo of the second kylix by Oltos in the Bareiss Collection. Inside, within a single reserved line, a bearded satyr runs to the right, holding a full wineskin before him and looking back over his shoulder. Instead of incising the details of the anatomy, the artist has drawn them in, using black relief lines for the contours and added red paint for the articulation of finer details like the creature's tail and his ivy wreath. The new technique produces a more easily readable rendering of the half-human figure.

In spite of the difference in technique, the two subjects are recognizably by the same artist—the running poses within the circular frames, the proportions of heads and bodies, and

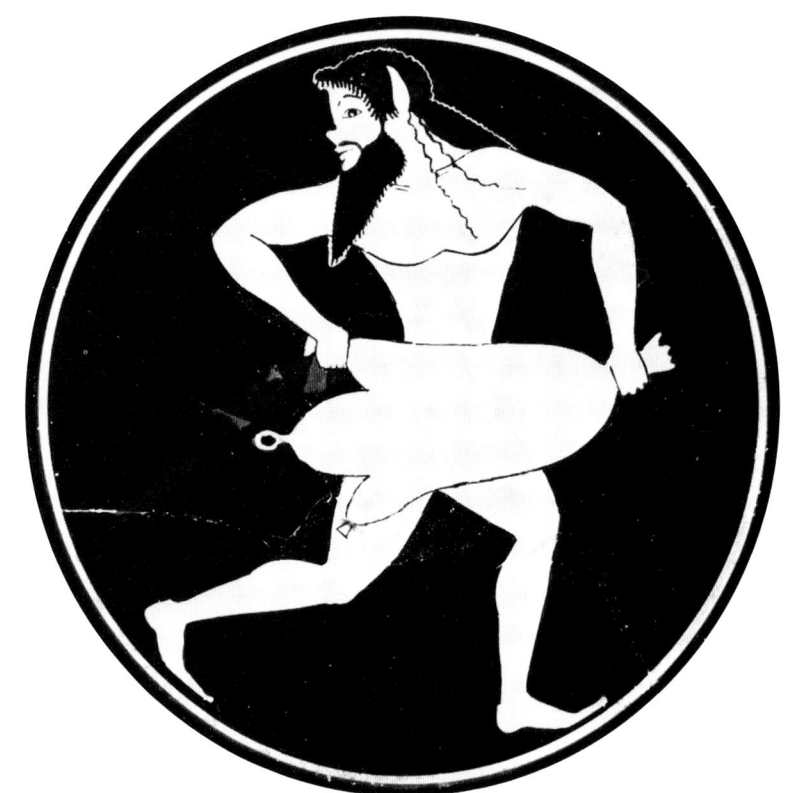

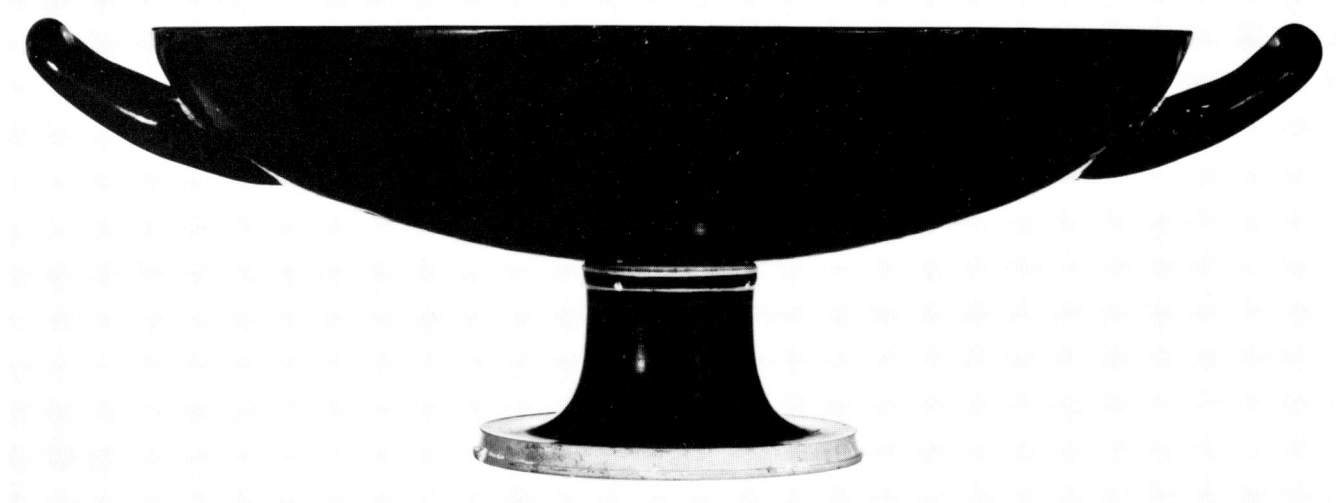

the husky, muscular figures drawn with a minimum of detail and maximum of exuberance are unmistakably the work of Oltos. Primarily a painter of cups, Oltos is known by name from two signatures found on his more than 150 surviving vases.

Aside from the employment of the two techniques side by side, the bilingual cup betrays its early date within the red-figure tradition through other details. The eyes on both sides had first been introduced by black-figure artists as a decorative feature for this particular shape of kylix. Exekias may have been responsible for the original conceit around 535 B.C. However, eye cups did not continue to be painted for much more than two decades after the switch to red-figure. Equally telling are the closed fronds of the palmettes, especially common in the work of Oltos; this feature does not continue much longer than the eyes, and even Oltos eventually spreads his fronds to form an open fan.

A word must also be said about the magnificent potting of both of these cups, for it is in its own way as readily attributable as the painting. The most telling detail, rarely visible when a vase is on exhibition, is the narrow raised edge which runs around the perimeter of each footplate's broad undersurface. The creator of this type of foot, which has a distinctive profile inside and out, is the potter Hischylos.

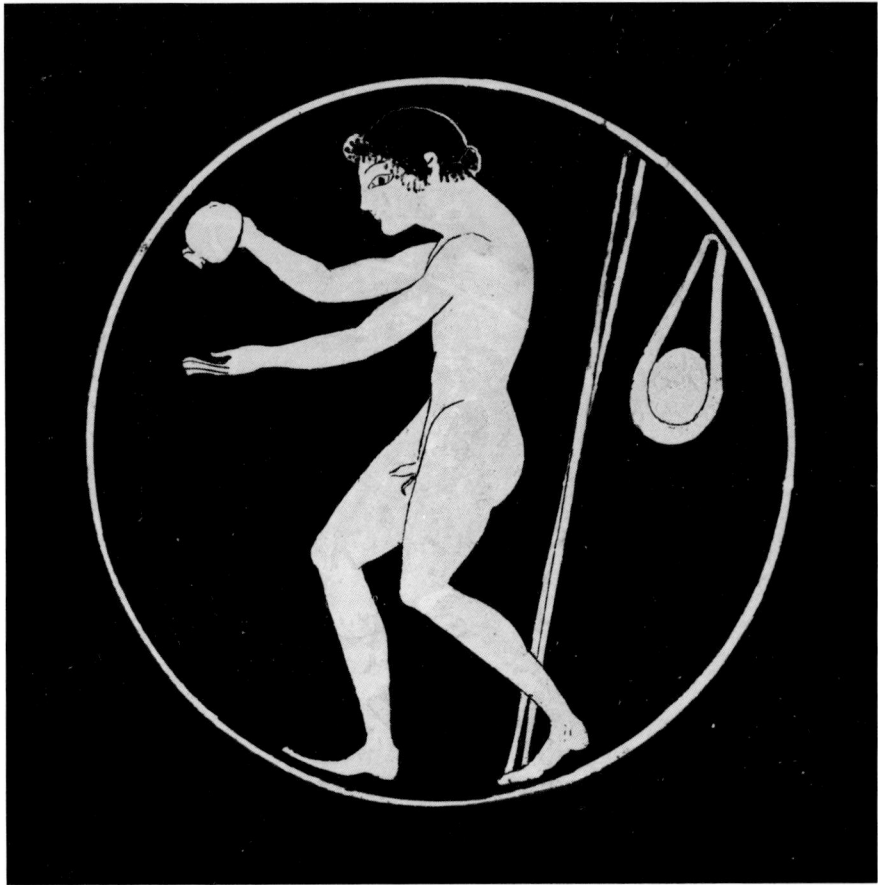

28. Cup Type C
Attributed to the Ambrosios Painter
Circa 510 B.C.
Height: 6.7 cm.
Diameter: 18.8 cm.
Checklist no. 165.

The Ambrosios Painter offers us a glimpse of the palaestra (the ancient Greek athletic field) within a simple reserved border in the tondo of this kylix. A young athlete has propped his javelins against the wall behind him, where his discus bag also hangs; and he stands to the left pouring oil from an aryballos into his open left palm. He will rub the oil on his nude body and then scrape it away with a strigil to clean off the dirt of the practice field. The exterior of the cup is undecorated.

This artist is neither a master of design nor a great draughtsman. Still, his little figure is spirited, and the composition, though unoriginal, quite pleasing. Named after the youth on the interior of his cup in Orvieto, the Ambrosios Painter specialized in cup decoration and, as Beazley noted, "if bad, he is never dull."

29. Cup Type B
Attributed to Epiktetos
Circa 510 B.C.
Height: 7.3 cm.
Diameter: 18 cm.
Checklist no. 145.

Beazley said of Epiktetos, "You cannot draw better, you can only draw differently." This artist combined superb draughtsmanship with an unerring sensitivity to composition to create some of the strongest, simplest vase paintings ever done; and this cup is a fine example of his work. In the center, a balding old man is happily accompanying himself on the lyre as he sings. Head thrown back, he is totally absorbed in his music. But, since he wears a komast's wreath, he is surely not singing for himself. This must be a figure abstracted from a symposion scene. Epiktetos is objective in his depiction here. He does not disguise the coarse features of the man's face or the receding hairline, but neither does he caricature his subject. Within the plain reserved circle that is his frame, he has given a straight-forward portrait of a man singing.

The shape of the tondo presents no problems for the artist; rather, he has used it to his advantage. The couch on which the musician reclines forms a level platform close to the bottom, but it is not a groundline. The edge of the singer's himation has slipped down into the otherwise empty exergue as a reminder that this is the space beneath the *kline*. The thin circle can barely contain its subject—a striped cushion is propped up against the frame on one side, the singer's left foot on the other. The resulting feeling that the performer is about to burst through his

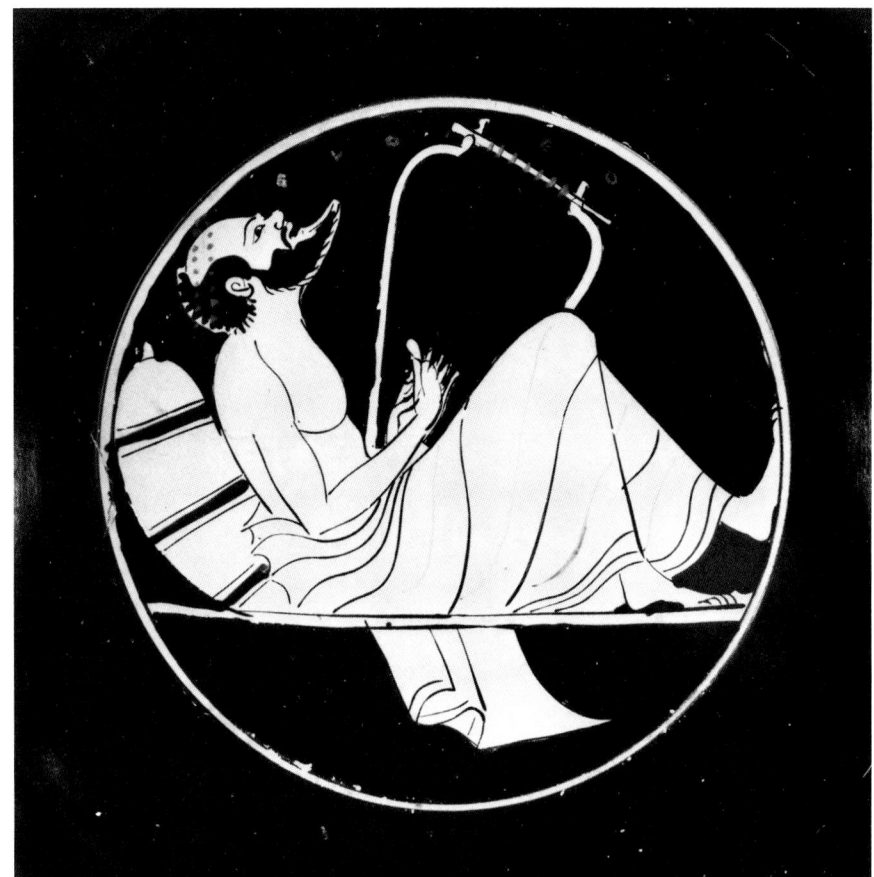

confines increases the powerful effect of the beautifully drawn figure.

Epiktetos' name is known from over forty signatures, and he signed once as both potter and painter. His career seems to end together with the sixth century B.C., but his uncluttered style was to influence greatly the generation of vase painters who followed him.

30. Cup Type B
Attributed to the Brygos Painter
Circa 490 B.C.
Diameter (est.): 31.6 cm.
Checklist no. 152.

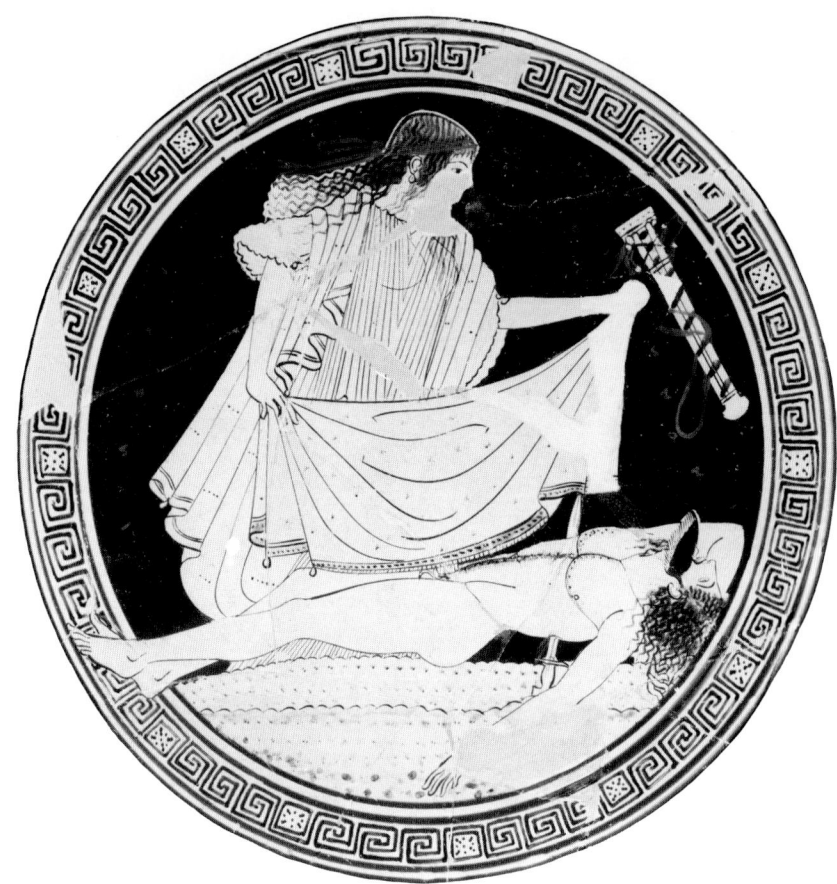

Primarily a painter of cups, the Brygos Painter had little interest in purely decorative patterns. Rather, he preferred to employ his fine draughtsmanship, originality, and intelligence in figural composition, of which the Bareiss cup is arguably his best.

In three scenes, he tells the entire story of the fall of one of the greatest of the Greek heroes, Aias. Aias, son of Telamon, risked his own life to save the body of Achilles from the Trojans. He assumed that the arms of the dead hero would be his reward. Others of the Greeks who participated in the same battle, most notably Odysseus, thought otherwise and managed to convince the leader, Agamemnon, that the arms should be awarded by contest. The two contenders, Aias and Odysseus, would present speeches explaining their claims to the arms. All of the Greek generals would then vote to choose between the two. The vote was taken by the casting of lots, and Odysseus won by one stone. Aias felt that his honor had been insulted publicly and was driven to madness by the goddess Athena. Finally, in despair, he killed himself by falling on his sword on a lonely stretch of beach.

On the exterior, the Brygos Painter has chosen the dispute between Aias and Odysseus to decorate one side, the casting of lots for the other. Filled with figures, these compositions are very carefully adapted to the difficult surface of the kylix, which provides much more room around the heads of the figures than at their feet. In the dispute, the protagonists are pulled away from one another, forming an open V-shaped composition which emphasizes the rift. The open spaces are filled with angry gestures and out-flung arms appropriate to such an emotional moment. In the voting scene, the dispute has been resolved. The table with the uneven piles of stones is central; and the final count is fifteen for Odysseus, who surely stands on the left with Athena, and fourteen for the dejected Aias, who stands isolated to the far right behind a tree, grieving with hand on head.

But it is the tondo which is the masterwork. Here within the circular maeander frame, the artist has brought his greatest strengths to his creation. The suicide of Aias was a popular theme in Greek vase painting from the seventh century B.C. onward. It was depicted by no less a master than the great black-figure artist Exekias. Yet the Brygos Painter has chosen an unusual moment for his composition. Not the moment of death, the personal tragedy, but the moment of the discovery, the public tragedy, is the subject. The shocked

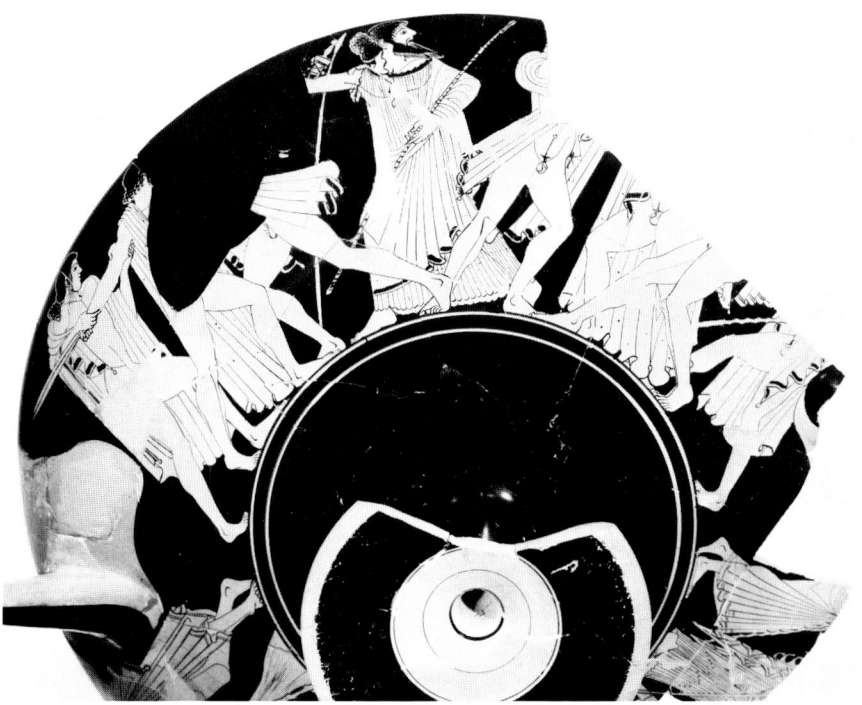

Tekmessa, Aias' beloved companion, runs to cover the body. Aias does not lie face down on his sword, as was traditional and also logical; rather he lies fully exposed on his back, the sword protruding from below his chest as if he were murdered from behind. The ground beneath the body is carefully described, with dilute washes and tiny dots to indicate the sandy and pebbly surface of the beach where the suicide took place. So concerned was the artist with the impact of his scene that the feet of Aias protrude into the maeander border which frames the composition.

The Brygos Painter was faithful to the Homeric legend and yet brilliant in his condensation of the story. He united the decoration of the entire vase with the three essential episodes skillfully adapted to the graceful bowl of the kylix.

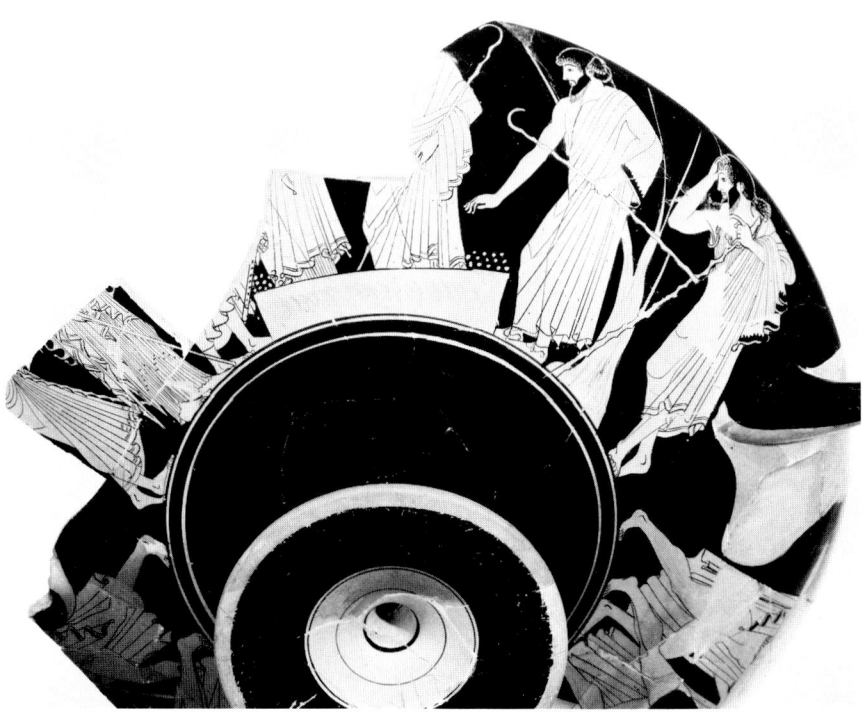

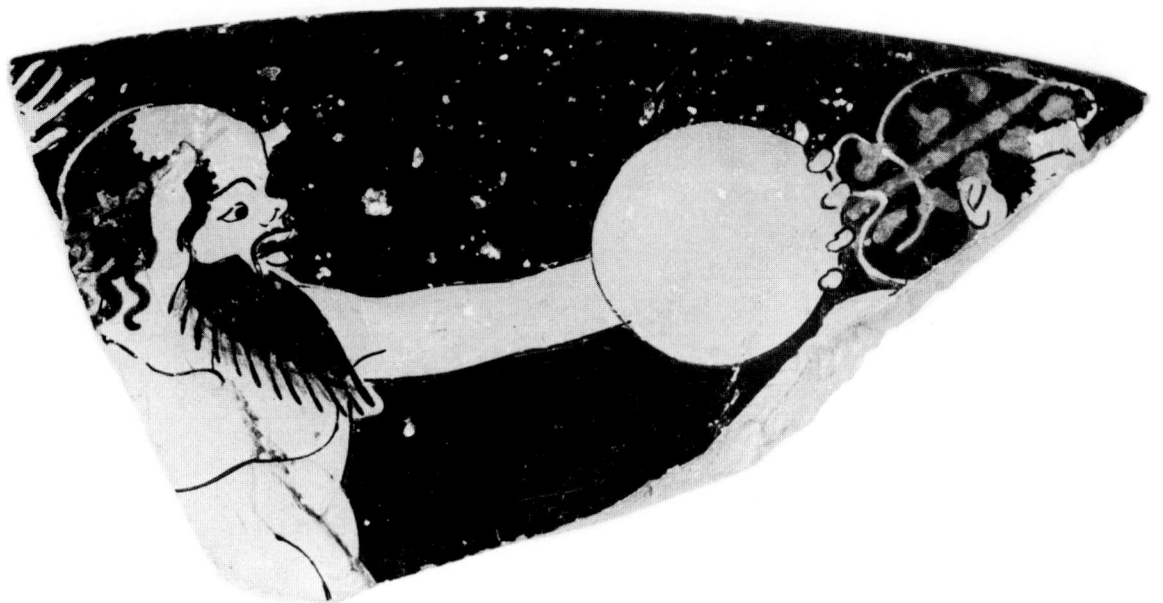

31. Cup Fragment
Attributed to the Brygos Painter
Circa 480 B.C.
Original diameter (est.): 28.2 cm.
Checklist no. 183.

The Brygos Painter often represented satyrs in various situations. On this fragment we have only the remains of two heads, but there is still enough to tell that a satyr stands to right behind Dionysos or a maenad, who looks off in the same direction. What is a little unusual here is the fact that the satyr holds up a discus, an object more appropriate to the palaestra than to the Dionysiac rites. Satyrs, the half-human, half-goat attendants of Dionysos, undergo some strange transformations during the early decades of red-figure vase painting, most probably under the influence of contemporary satyr plays. They become progressively more human in form on the vases of the later sixth century. Only their tails (more horse-like than goatish), little horns, and coarse facial features consistently distinguish them, though some artists do make them hairy. They also begin to participate in human activities other than revelry and love-making. They put on helmets, carry shields, and take part in athletics. The Brygos Painter evidently found it impossible to believe that a satyr could be single-mindedly devoted to sports and included at least a second companion from the Bacchic revels.

32. Cup Type B
Attributed to the Briseis Painter
Signed by the potter Brygos
Circa 480-470 B.C.
Height: 11.6 cm.
Diameter: 30.8 cm.
Checklist no. 159.

On the inside of one of the handles of this cup is painted a very important inscription: BRVΛOS EΓOIESEN ("Brygos made it"). This is the signature of the potter who gives his name to the so-called Brygos Painter. However, the cup is not the work of this painter but of one of his companions.

Beazley divided the followers of the Brygos Painter into three groups. The Briseis Painter is the primary representative of the group called Mild-Brygan. Although many details in this artist's style recall the best works of his master, the overall impression of his work lacks the vitality of the Brygos Painter at his best. The sweetness and calm that distinguish the interior courting scene of this cup, with a youth offering a flower to a rather uninterested girl who stands holding her mirror, are typical of the Briseis Painter.

On the outside, a party of ten men and youths dressed up as women and one female attendant dance around the entire circumference. Some partici-

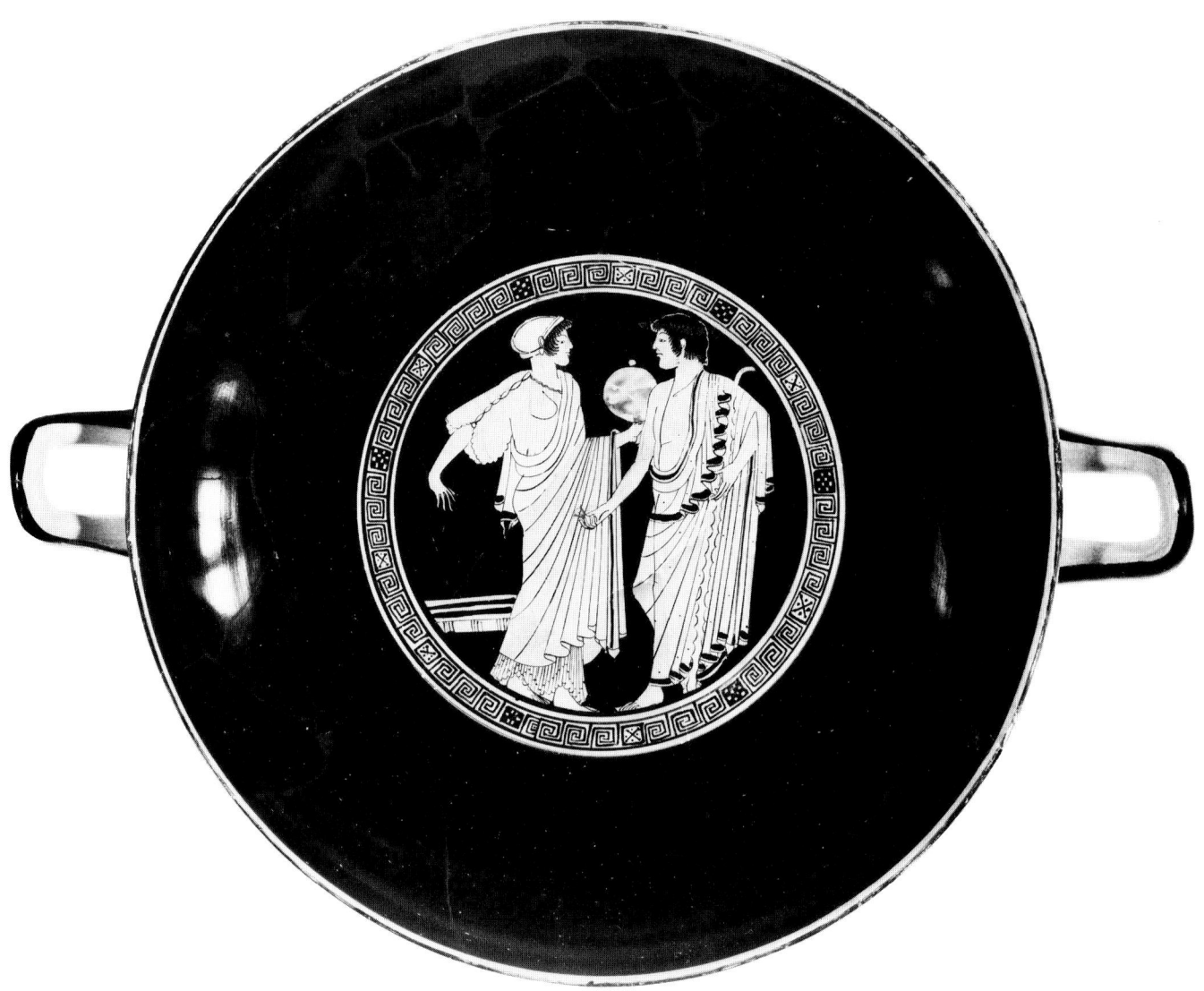

pants carry wine cups, two provide the music for the dance with their flutes, two others play *krotala* (castanets), and the girl and one older figure (the head is missing) hold up parasols to shelter the other dancers. The only interruptions in the general rightward movement are the parasol carrier who is turned to the left beside one handle (A/B) and the large column krater under the other, signed handle (B/A), which not only holds the wine but also determines the beginning and end of the composition. Such transvestites are fairly common subjects on vases in the late sixth and early fifth centuries B.C. Since at least three vases survive with one of these figures inscribed: ANAKPEON, Beazley interpreted the groups as the poet Anakreon and his boon companions. He dismissed the idea that the scenes might represent religious rites or a festival, since the figures are often drinking or carrying wine cups. Anakreontists appear again in the Bareiss Collection on the exterior of his cup by the Sabouroff Painter (Checklist no. 162) and on his fragment from a stemless cup by a follower of Douris (Checklist no. 191).

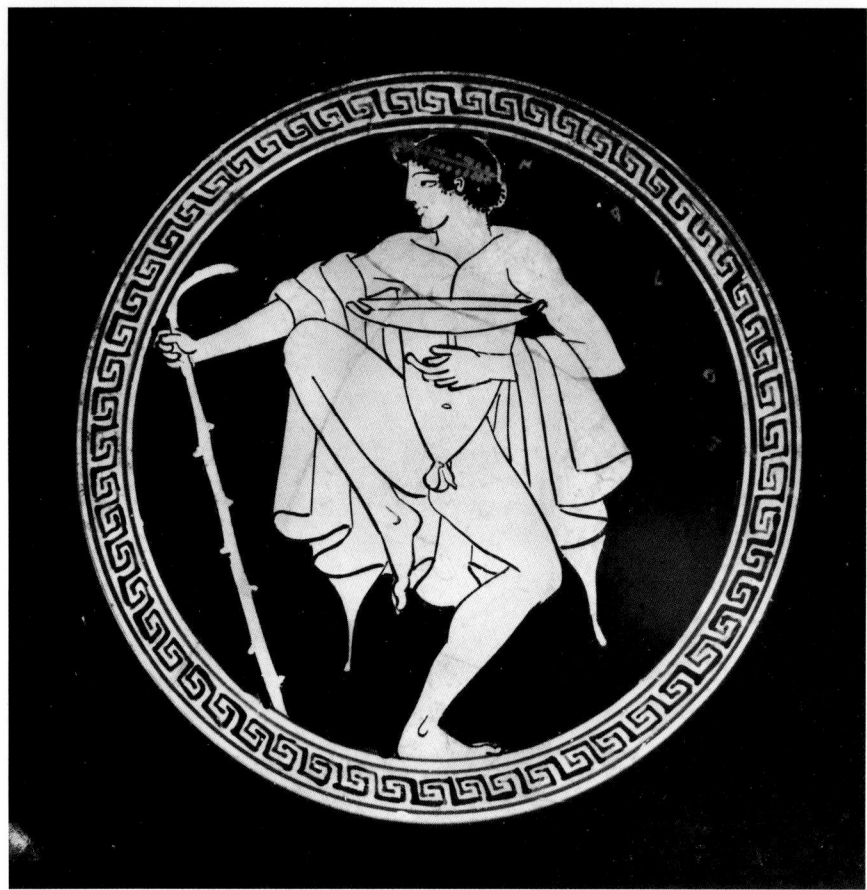

33. Cup Type B
Attributed to the Painter Makron
Circa 480-470 B.C.
Height: 7.9 cm.
Diameter: 19.4 cm.
Checklist no. 158.

Decorating the circular tondo of a kylix presented unique problems for vase painters. The most difficult was to find a means of posing upright figures convincingly inside the curving frame. Various solutions presented themselves—the use of a groundline within the tondo, the choice of a moving figure with legs spread as the subject, or the acceptance of awkward, tilted poses. Certainly one of the most graceful and creative solutions is found in the tondo of this cup by Makron. A youthful reveler balances his weight without effort on one outturned foot and a walking stick. With both knees and one elbow bent, one arm outstretched, and a mantle that moves with the dance steps, his frontal figure expansively fills the center. His wreathed head is in profile to the left within the upper arc of the tondo. The inscription, ΚΑLΟS ("Beautiful") is added in red in the upper right field. A master of the late archaic period, Makron here delights in the freedom with which artists could now represent the active human figure.

The artist left the exterior of this cup undecorated, concentrating our attention on the graceful, unbroken return curve of the profile. Interest in the kylix as a shape is further emphasized by the vase which the komast somehow manages to hold level as he dances.

34. Cup Type B
Signed by the Painter Douris
Potted by Python
Circa 480 B.C.
Height: 11.8 cm.
Diameter: 30.1 cm.
Checklist no. 156.

Within the tondo of this well-preserved cup, the tall, straight figure of a bearded man stands before a youth who is heavily muffled in a himation. The youth carries a tortoise-shell lyre, and the man is perhaps his music teacher. The season may be winter. Two pairs, each a youth and a man, appear on either side of the exterior, though here the youths are seated while the men stand. At the right end of each side stands a third man. Lyres hang on the wall behind the figures along with string bags for knucklebones, and sponges and aryballoi used in athletics. One youth on side B has a hare on his lap, and the central man on side A offers one to his young pupil. Since this animal is a traditional Greek love gift, its appearance here twice suggests that the scenes depict courting as well as instruction in the classroom setting.

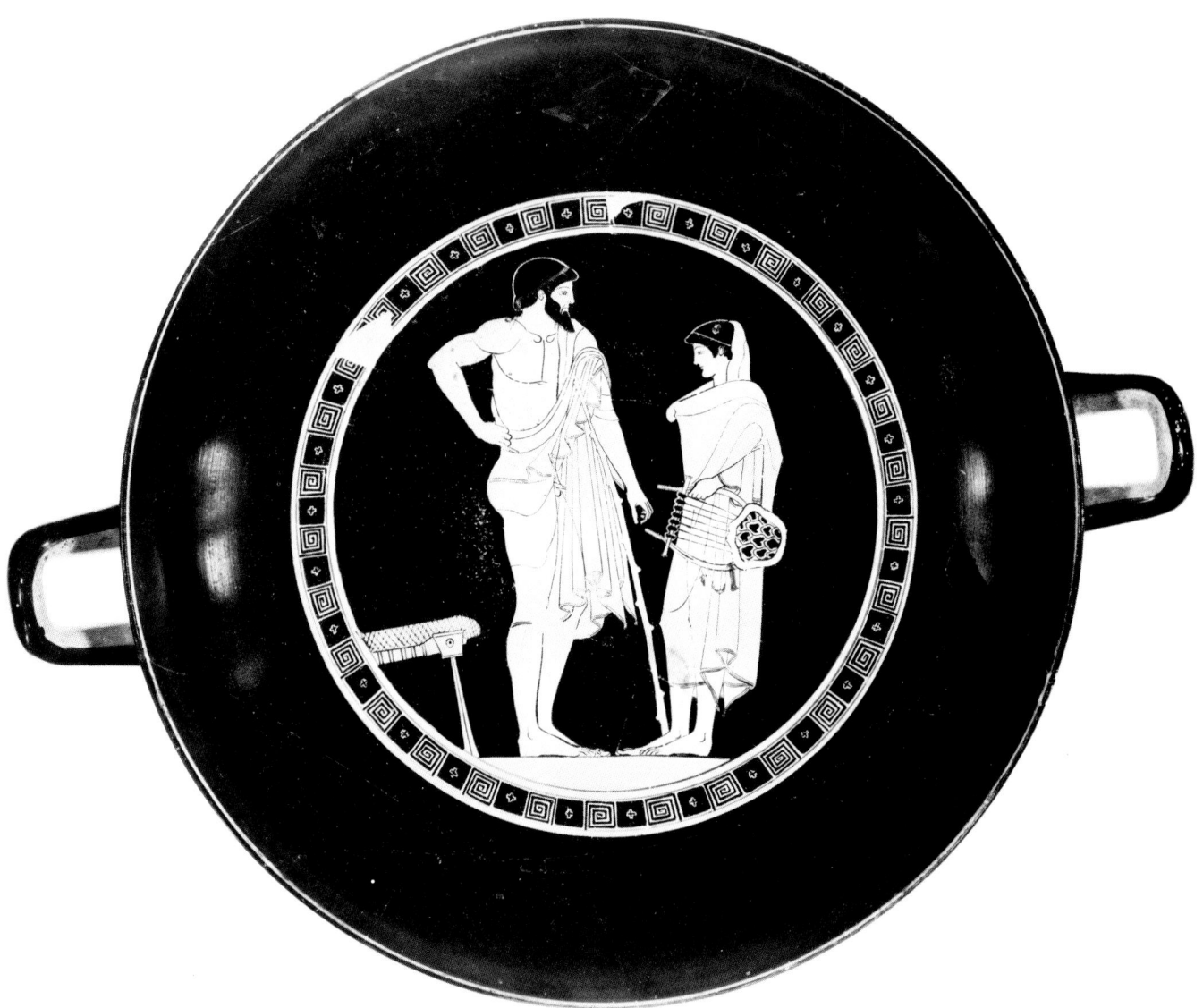

The cup is signed around the tondo figures: ΔORIS [E]ΓRAΦSEN ("Douris painted it"). This contemporary of the Brygos Painter and Makron often signed his name on his work. However, he used two different forms of delta in his signature at different times, thus providing a clue to the chronology of his vases. In his earlier works, he used a standard delta, Δ only later did he switch to the Samian form, Λ, which appears here.

Twice on the outside is inscribed, HIΠOΔAMAS KAΛOS. Another good indicator for chronology, this love name frequently appears on the mature works of Douris, associated by Beazley with the third of his four periods. To this period also belongs the liberal use of floral decoration, so well represented by the magnificent palmettes at the handles of this cup, and the characteristic border of single false maeander squares alternating with crossed squares around the tondo.

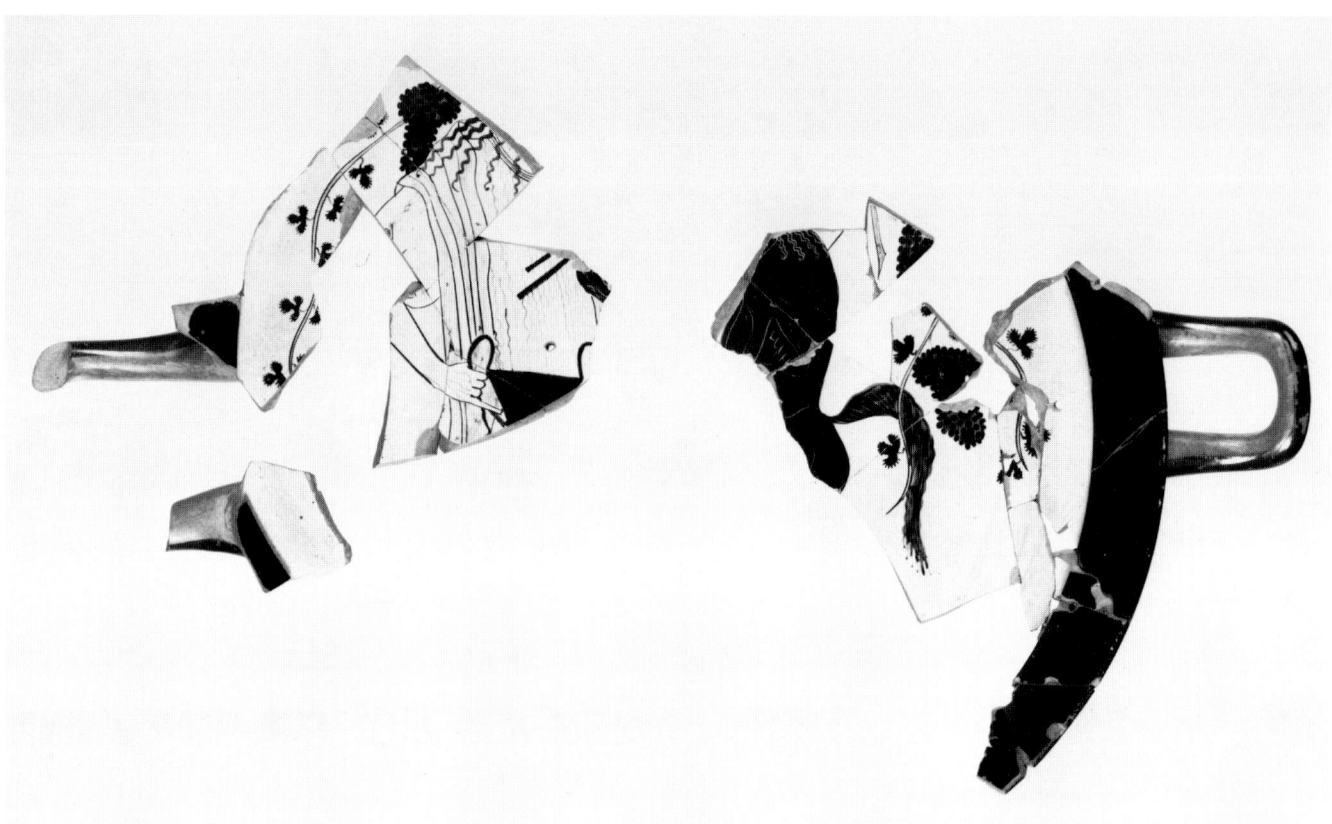

Douris frequently collaborated with the potter Python, who has not signed here, but to whom this cup has been attributed by Bothmer. The profile of the foot, especially underneath, is distinctly his work.

35. White-ground Cup Fragments (Lipped inside)
Attributed to Onesimos
Potted by Euphronios
Circa 490 B.C.
Diameter (est.): 23.6 cm.
Checklist no. 181.

These few fragments from an Attic drinking cup, more than any other piece in the Bareiss Collection, remind us of how much ancient art has been lost. The potter was Euphronios, the painter, Onesimos, and the result of their collaboration, a masterpiece. The exterior was left completely black; but inside, the black offset lip framed a bowl completely covered with whitish slip. On this pale surface, the artist drew two figures whose approximate appearances can be reconstructed from the remains. Dionysos stood on the left. Painted in outline, he wears a finely pleated chiton, buttoned down the sleeve, with a heavier, patterned mantle over his shoulders. He holds a kantharos painted in black silhouette in his right hand. He faces a satyr painted in black who stands beside him on the right playing the double flutes. Bunches of grapes and grapevines, which may have sprung from a branch in the god's missing hand, fill the background.

In black-figure vase painting, the use of white-ground created a greater contrast between background and figures but did not change the basic concept of a dark figure on a light ground (see, for example, the kyathos, above No. 16). With white-ground at the time of red-figure, the situation is somewhat different. Although the figure may be drawn in the same manner on the white slip as it would have been on the red body of a vase, it is no longer offset by a dark background. Instead, it has become a light figure on a light ground, a situation which focuses all our attention on the draughtsmanship. The technique is called semi-outline. In this cup, Onesimos seems actually to have combined something of both the black- and red-figure techniques, with Dionysos in outline and the satyr completely black.

The painter worked here with no additional color; he simply used the black glaze in various degrees of dilution to create the paler yellowish tones and in a very viscous state for the relief lines and the bunches of grapes. Yet, the coloristic and textural effects achieved within this very limited range of colors are still remarkable, in spite of the very fragmentary condition of the cup.

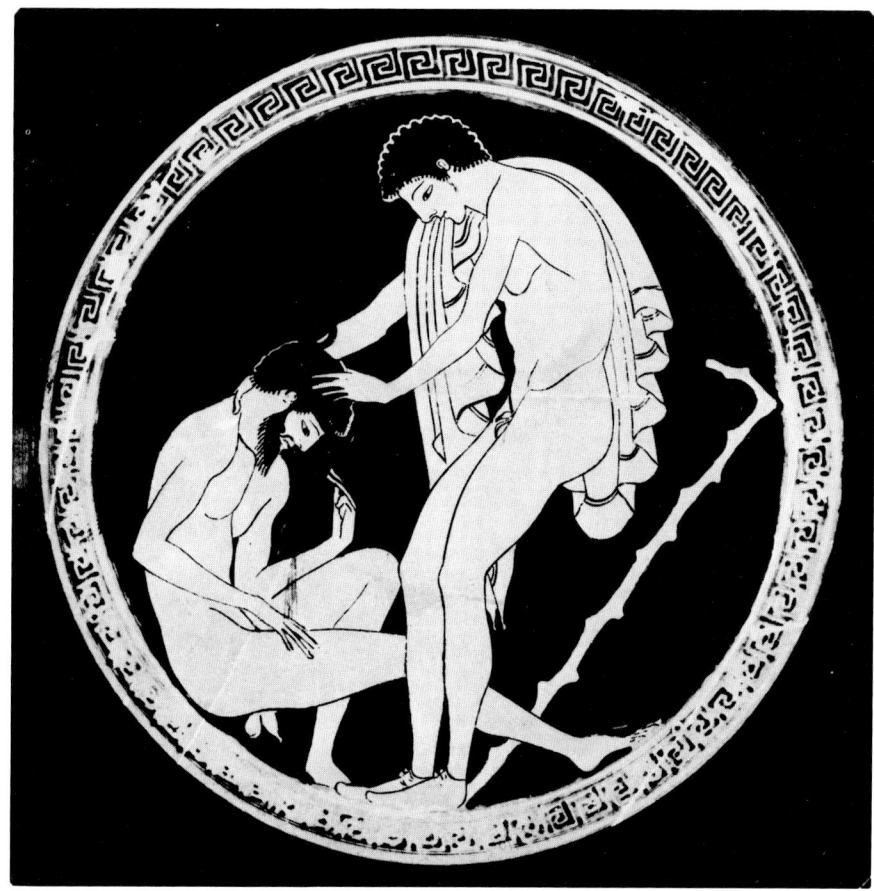

36. Cup Type B, Fragmentary
Attributed to Onesimos
Circa 500 B.C.
Diameter (est.): 23.6 cm.
Checklist no. 150.

37. Cup Type B
Attributed to Onesimos
Signed by Euphronios as potter
Circa 490 B.C.
Diameter (tondo): 14 cm.
Checklist no. 151.

A cup (the Greek word is *kylix*) was made for drinking, and the classical Greeks enjoyed wine no less than today's Californians. But the cups were rather voluminous, thus it is no wonder that people got drunk easily, even if the usual (and economical) custom was to drink wine mixed with a good deal of water. The consequences of immoderate drinking were a favorite subject for decoration of drinking cups. As a deterrent? Most certainly not; rather as a sample of good humor.

The inside medallions of both cups show a bearded man who has drunk more than was good for him. In one case (No. 36), he is all alone in his distress, bending over his stick; in the

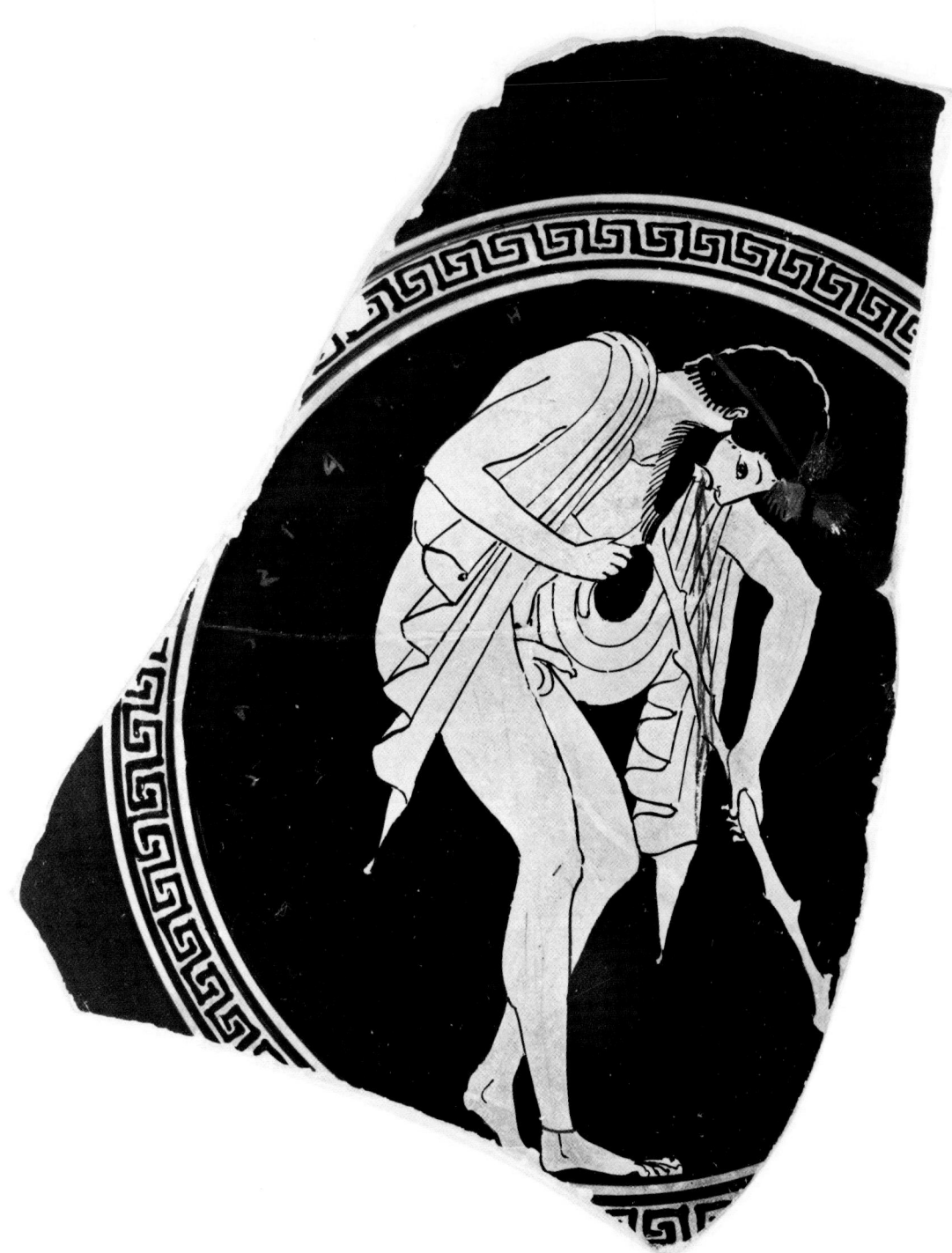

other (No. 37), a young friend is holding his head. But the most interesting feature is the way of relating the unfortunate consequences of overindulgence. The inexperienced eye does not at first notice the tiny stream of added red indicating the flow of the wine which refuses to stay in the drinker's stomach. And the drinker looks as if nothing were happening—he remains idealized with the good looks and calm demeanor considered suitable for representations of Greeks and their gods; one could say that he is vomiting like a hero. The subtle humor of the scene avoids any vulgarity.

The same is true for the representations on the outside of both cups. Love is the natural companion of drinking. Thus on No. 37 two revelers approach a girl on each side. One girl is drinking too; the other is playing castanets. Both are at the party not as guests but as entertainers. In the representation of the female nude, the otherwise accomplished painter seems to have failed: the girls, with their wide shoulders and narrow hips, look a little like boys with added breasts. This was the accepted convention of the time, which preferred the beauty of well-articulated male proportions to female softness. Of the outside of the No. 36, only fragments are preserved; they show couples making love. For the Greeks there was no embarrassment in such scenes.

It is evident, even to the novice observer, that both cups were decorated by the same hand. The name of the painter is known. Onesimos preferred to decorate cups, and many of them were thrown by the famous Euphronios; indeed, No. 37 is signed by Euphronios as potter. By the end of the sixth century, Euphronios gave up painting. Perhaps his eyesight was failing, or perhaps he succeeded in acquiring a pottery workshop. However, he was as outstanding as a potter as he was as a vase painter; the profiles of these cups are of masterful perfection. His influence as a painter persisted, however, in the work of his students; it can be detected in Onesimos' drawing.

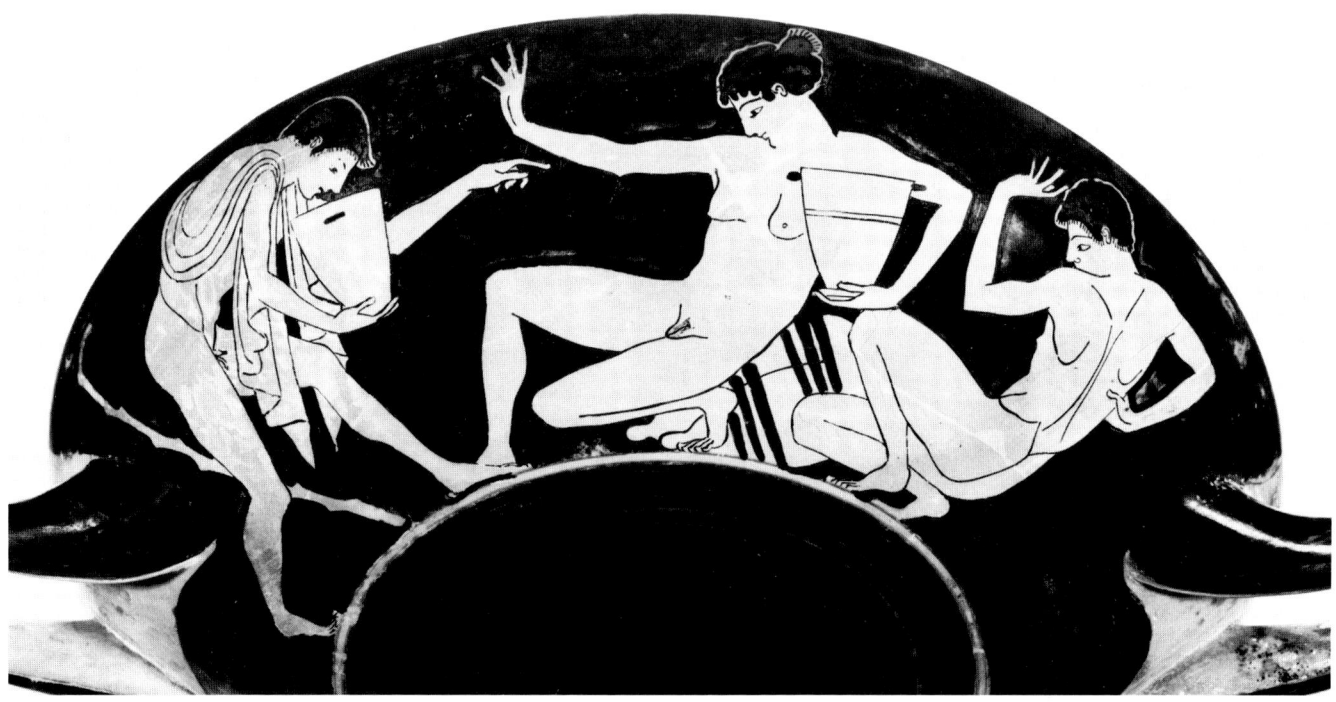

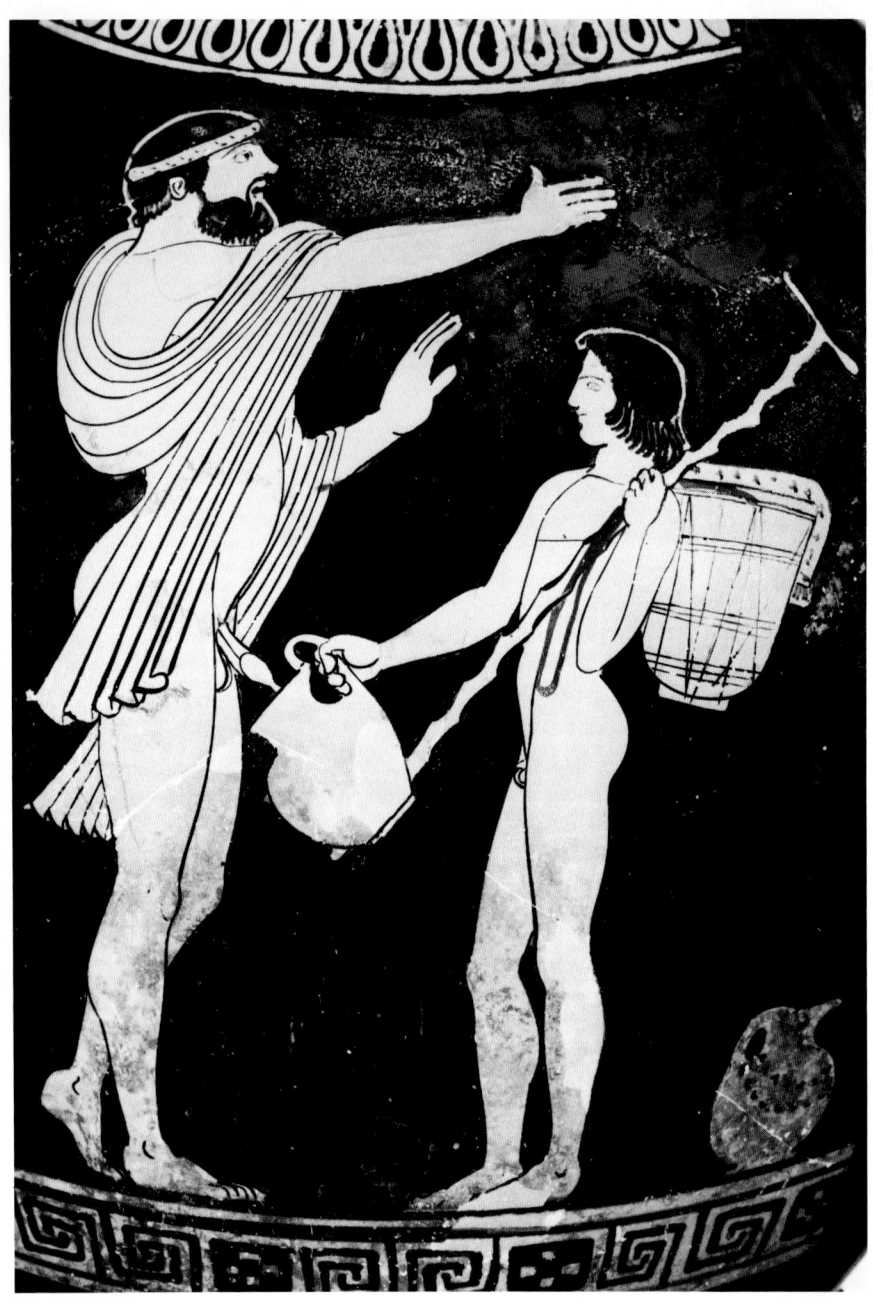

38. Oinochoe, Shape 3 (chous)
Circa 470 B.C.
Height: 23.5 cm.
Checklist no. 119.

Juglets of this shape with trefoil mouths were called choes (sing.: chous) already in antiquity. The same word also meant a measure of liquid, say, of wine, thus perhaps a quantity for competitive drinking. Smaller choes were used for a measure of wine for a child on the day also named *choes*, a festival in early spring for sampling new wine and commemorating the dead.

The scene on the Bareiss chous is closely connected with wine drinking. A bearded man, with a short mantle stretched forward over his arms, betrays by his gesture and insecure stance that he has drunk more than a safe measure. His bladder too may be overstretched, and he is not fully aware of it. Luckily his small male servant, carrying his master's stick and a basket of food covered by a cloth, understands the situation. He tenders a jug (similar to a chous, but without the trefoil mouth) to relieve his master. They must have just left a drinking party, symbolized by the chous decorated with wreaths on the ground behind the boy.

39. Skyphos
Circa 470-460 B.C.
Height: 15.3 cm.
Diameter: 18.8 cm.
Checklist no. 138.

This drinking cup presents a rather unusual image from everyday life. The description may start exceptionally with the secondary side, where a still life is represented. Two ladles and a jug hang on a metal stand; above is a big skyphos, and below stands a metal bail amphora with a hinged handle. A curious feature appears in the middle of the picture. At first one might think it is a grill hanging on the wall with a lidded casserole above it; but an ingenious interpretation has been proposed by D. von Bothmer: it is the grilled window of the cellar. At the right, a pointed storage amphora for wine is leaning against a chest used as a stand for a smaller casket and a chous crowned with wreaths.

On the obverse are two people who have just left the cellar. A small maid walks behind, carrying a one-handled amphora and a wineskin. Her face shows serious embarrassment: her mistress, walking in front, is guzzling from a large skyphos, a replica of the one in the cellar. Evidently, some Athenian housewives of the fifth century B.C. indulged in drinking no less than their husbands.

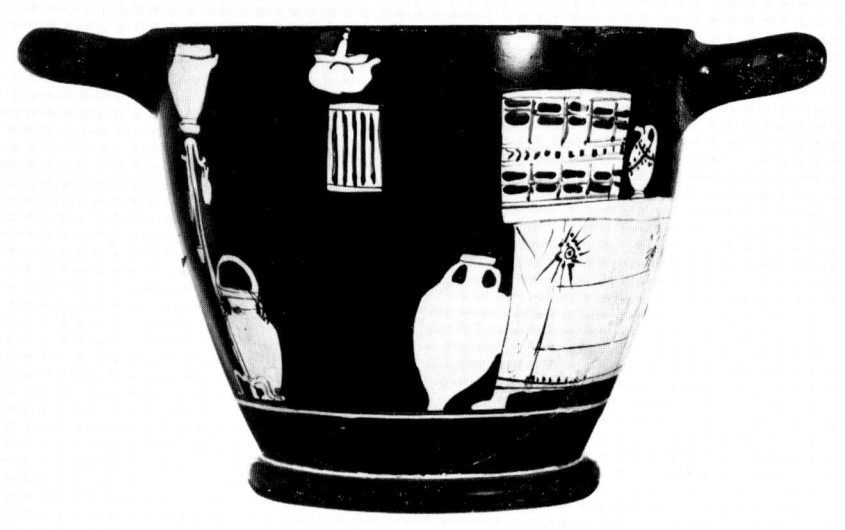

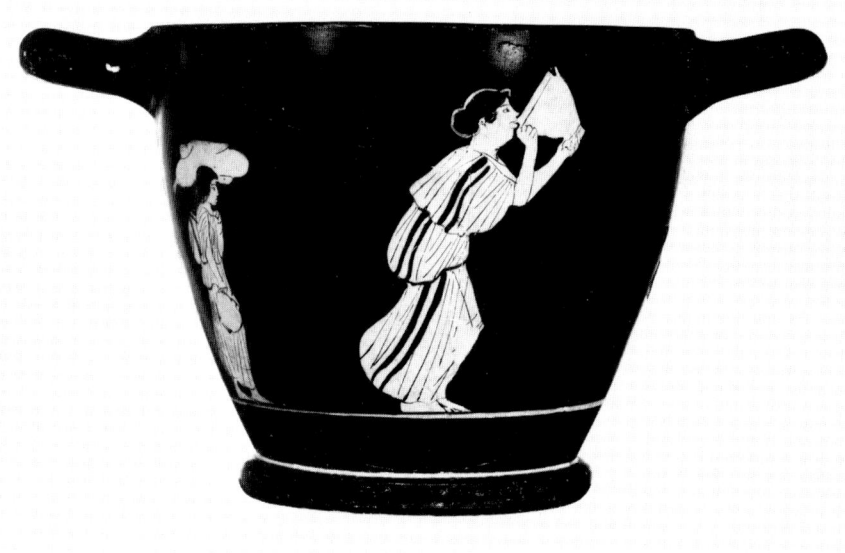

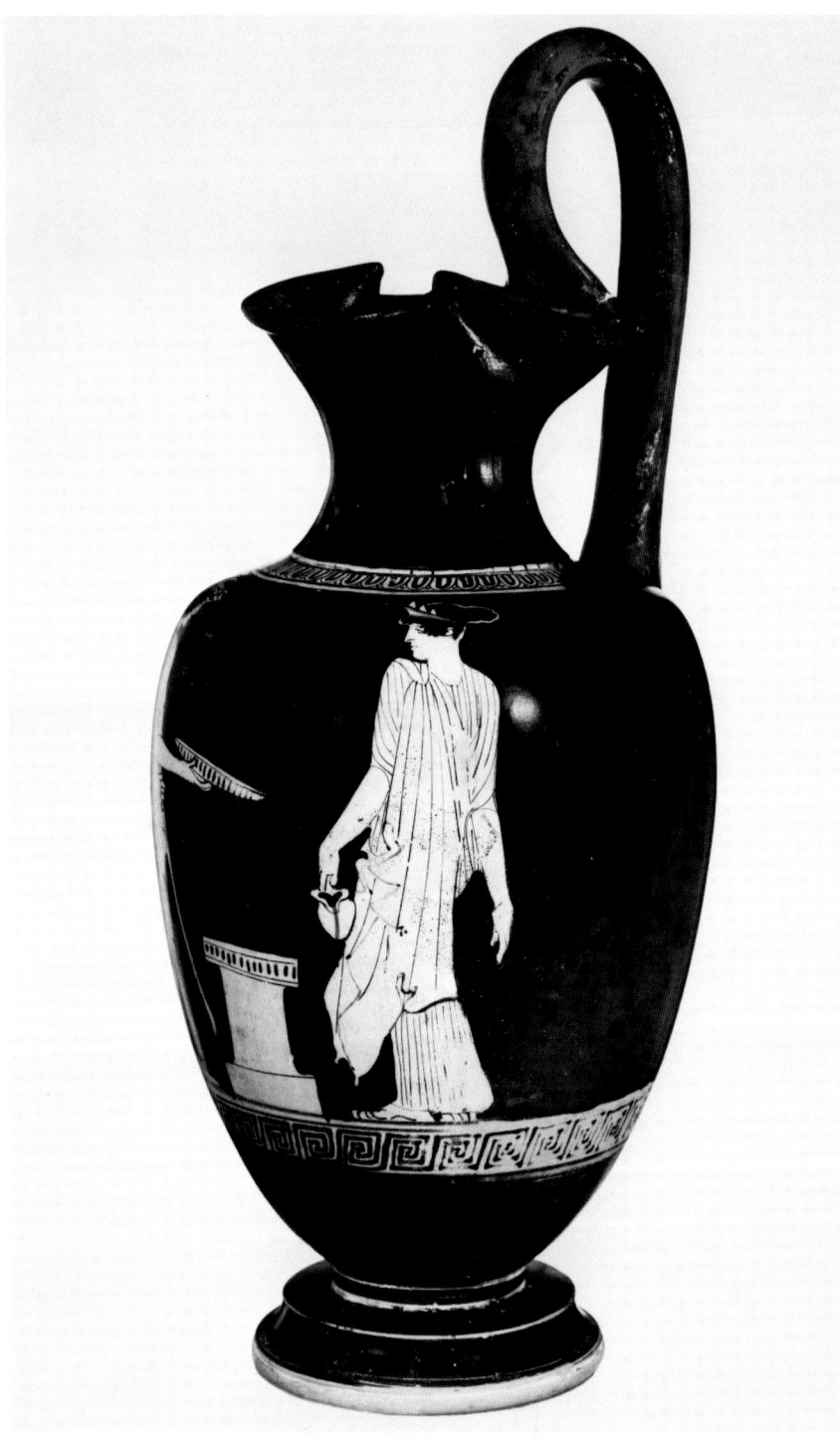

40. Trefoil Oinochoe, Shape 1
Attributed to the Richmond Painter
Circa 440 B.C.
Height (with handle): 28.8 cm.
Checklist no. 118.

On the front of this oinochoe the Richmond Painter has depicted Apollo and Artemis sacrificing at a low altar. The twins, inscribed ΚΑΛΟΣ and ΚΑΛΕ ("Beautiful," male and female), can be recognized by their attributes. On other vases by the same artist, these same basic figure types are often slightly altered to represent two men, two women, or two other gods. The figural decoration is the least interesting aspect of this vase, as it is of most vases by this artist. He continuously repeats a few stock figures for the decoration of all his vases. Nor does his lack of originality have the apology that the artist was concentrating his energies on the highly original potting or that his interests were in the production of vases of extremely high quality.

Rather, the repetitive quality is the result of the mass-production of vases. The Richmond Painter was part of a fairly large pottery workshop active in the third quarter of the fifth century B.C. The shop must have produced much of its work for export to the Etruscan market since many examples have been found in Italian soil. The vases themselves suggest that there was a division of labor among the potters, as individual vase parts—the mouth, the foot, and the body—were interchangeable with other vase shapes from the same workshop (see Checklist Nos. 98 and 99). An amphora potted by the same

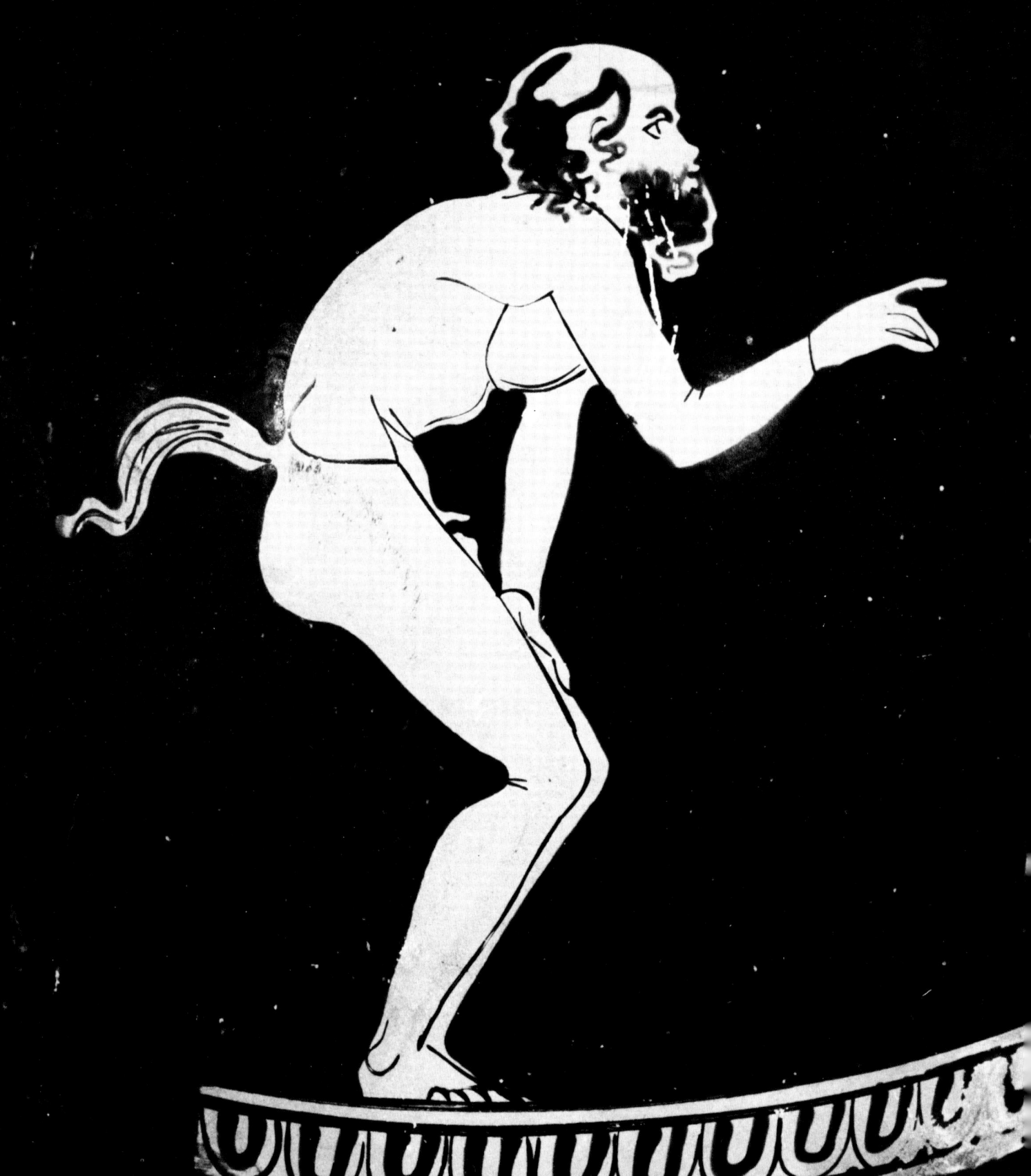

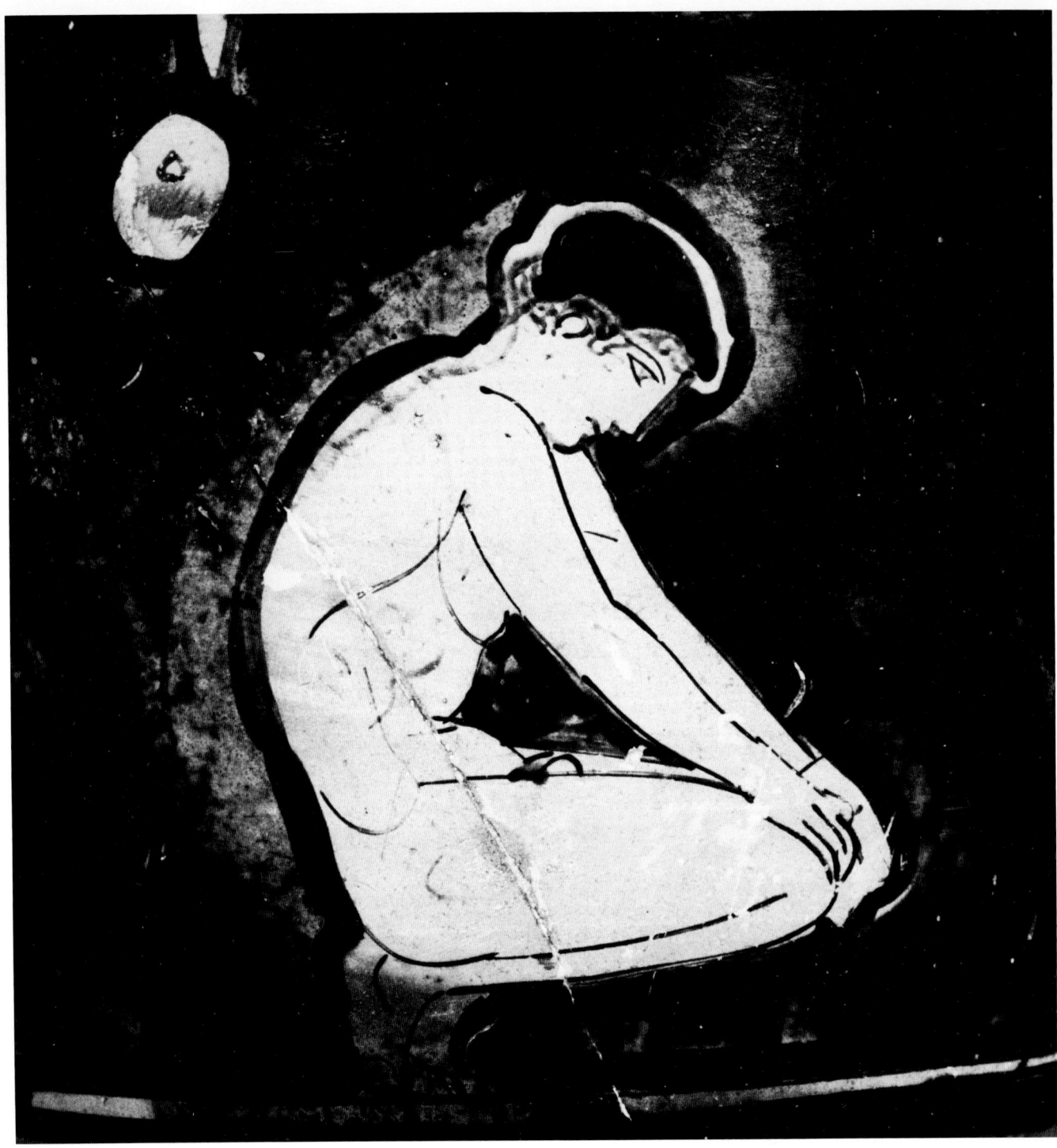

hand as this oinochoe has exactly the same body and foot; only the neck and handles are different. The painters also specialized, some in figure scenes and others in the decorative patterns. Apparently, the market created in Italy during the late sixth and early fifth centuries B.C. continued to demand large quantities of Greek ceramics fifty years later, even though the quality of production had declined in Athens—partially the result of increased wealth permitting more common use of metal vessels. Artists no longer took delight in the challenge of the curved surfaces of the various shapes, and the shapes themselves were standardized for easier production.

41. Squat Lekythos
Attributed to the Eretria Painter
Circa 430-420 B.C.
Height: 16.5 cm.
Checklist no. 133.

42. Oinochoe, Shape 8C (Mug)
Attributed to the Eretria Painter
Circa 430-420 B.C.
Height: 8.7 cm.
Checklist no. 123.

Beazley called the Eretria Painter an "exquisite miniaturist." Although he seems to have been primarily a cup painter, his best work appears on small pots, like this lekythos and mug, whose proportions and profiles suit his dainty figures. On the lekythos (No. 41) is a composition that parodies the myth of Oedipus. A playful satyr stands talking to a sphinx seated on a high perch. The subject, treated with great seriousness by earlier vase painters, has now become a comic satyr play. And, just as the artist's attitude toward his subject is playful and free, so is his drawing. The curves of the satyr's head and back and of the back of the sphinx subtly repeat the profile of the lekythos body. The satyr's hair and beard, the little curl at the end of his tail, the momentary gesture of his right hand, and the sphinx's wings are all rapidly sketched. Relief lines are used to define the major contours of both bodies, but they are applied sparingly and quickly, especially on the hands of the satyr and the wing of the sphinx. Dilute glaze markings are applied with even greater haste.

The same spontaneity is found in the figure of the young athlete on the oinochoe (No. 42). With a few sure lines the artist has captured the pose of the boy squatting with his hands on his knees, his weight on the balls of his feet. The see-saw on which he stands is a slanting reserved line, and the aryballos suspended on the wall behind is indicated with as little effort as possible. A few details, like the hair around the face, the iris of the eye, and the muscles of the torso and thigh, are simply suggested with dilute glaze.

The Eretria Painter was one of the most influential artists of the classical period, and his work illustrates very well the changing interests of the late-fifth-century vase painters. He chose to draw elegant figures in small-scale, often in elaborate compositions. However, his economical, confident use of relief lines and his swiftly applied dilute glaze details add a freshness to his subjects that prevents their becoming too precious. His best vase paintings are at once rich and free.

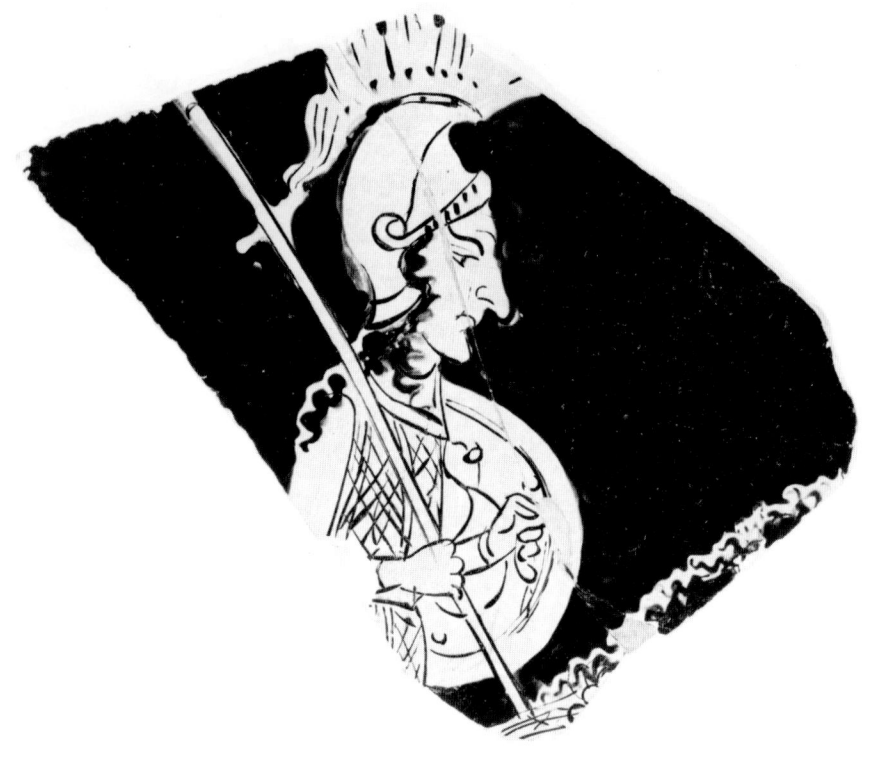

43. Bell Krater Fragment
Circa 375 B.C.
Height: 12 cm.
Checklist no. 223.

What remains from the scene on the side of a large vessel for mixing wine is a bust of the fully-armed goddess Athena bending slightly over another figure (Cassandra?). While the scene cannot be identified, the intention of the painter is evident. The goddess of wisdom, who did not hesitate to compete with Aphrodite in a beauty contest, is depicted as an ugly old woman, with crooked nose and emaciated face.

Was the painter being disrespectful to the goddess? The Homeric gods were already described as able to laugh at themselves; and not long after the *Iliad* and *Odyssey* were written down, the War of Frogs and Mice parodied them. In vase painting, the first grotesque figures appear toward the middle of the seventh century B.C., although accomplished caricatures date only from the very late sixth. But the most successful creations of this genre were achieved by the Greeks in South Italy in the fourth century, the date of the Bareiss fragment.

44. Bell Krater Fragment
Attributed to the Black Fury Group
Ca. 390-380 B.C.
Height: 19 cm.
Checklist no. 221.

As the quality of Attic vase painting declined in the second half of the fifth century B.C., the cities of Magna Graecia (Southern Italy) began to produce local wares in imitation of

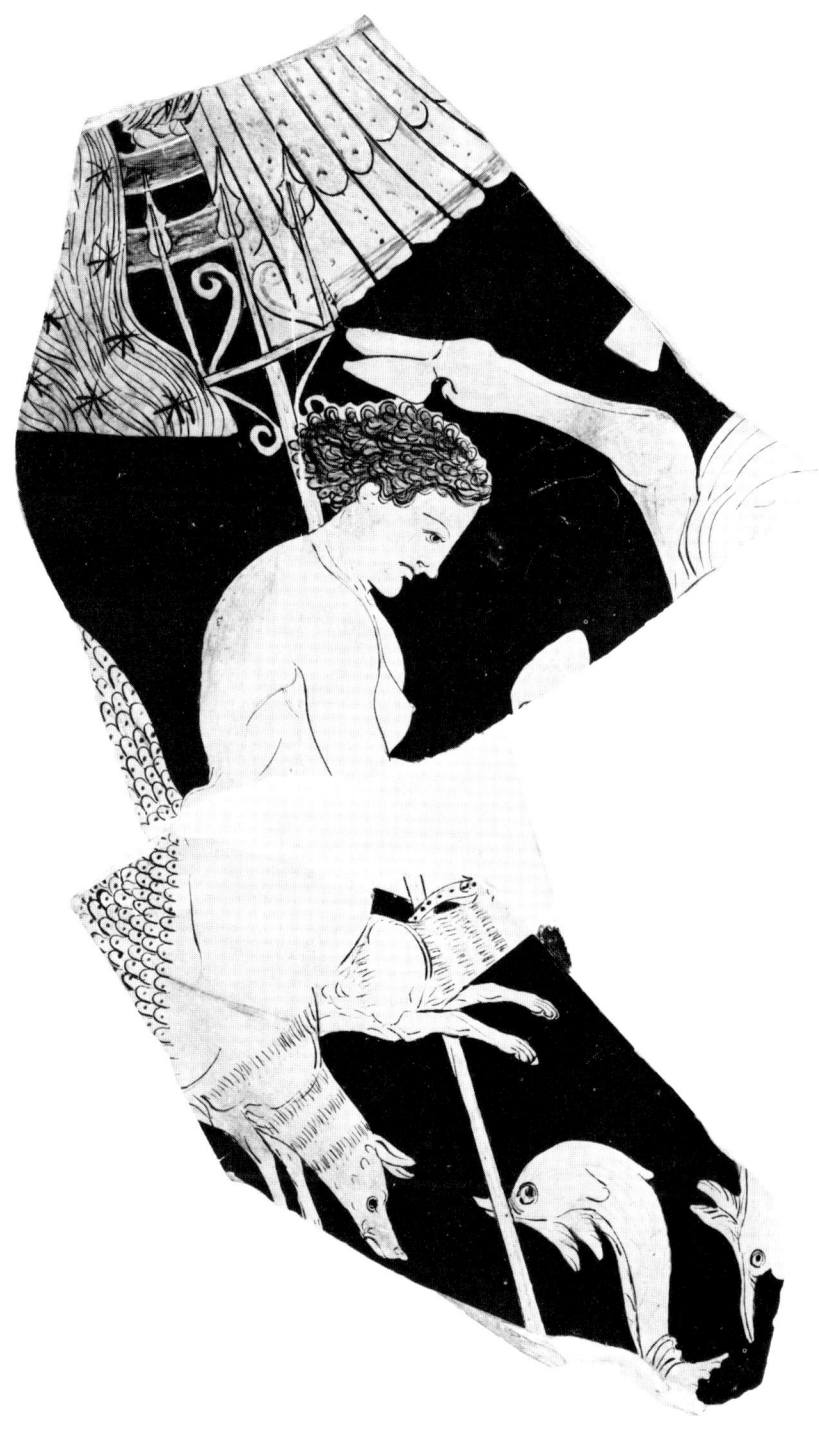

the popular Greek imports to satisfy the appetite for red-figure pottery. At first the artists may actually have been immigrants from the Greek workshops. Finally, the Peloponnesian War (431-404 B.C.) put an end to the vase trade between Athens and the west, and local centers of production took control of the Italian market.

Distinct differences between the Greek models and the Italian products quickly developed. The clays of South Italy were not as fine as those of Attica, and they fired to a paler color. And, since local tastes dictated the choices of subject and composition, myths of particular interest to the area, sometimes quite obscure, began to appear, often in designs of non-Greek complexity. Still, the drawing could be very fine, as this splendid fragment from an Apulian krater demonstrates.

Scylla, the many-headed sea monster who, according to legend, plagued sailors in the straits between Sicily and the toe of the Italian boot, here swims in the ocean. She holds a conch shell in her right hand; and a trident, attribute of all marine spirits, rests against her left shoulder. Dolphins leap in the water in front of her. Above, on the left, part of a wing and some fine drapery patterned with stars remain from another mythical creature, and the right foreleg and the chest of a bull are in the upper right field. The story of the Rape of Europa was popular in the Greek colonies, and this Scylla may well have been a mere accessory figure in such a scene. Even so, the artist has taken pains to suggest the various textures of her scales, her hair, and the short fur on the dogs' heads at her hips.

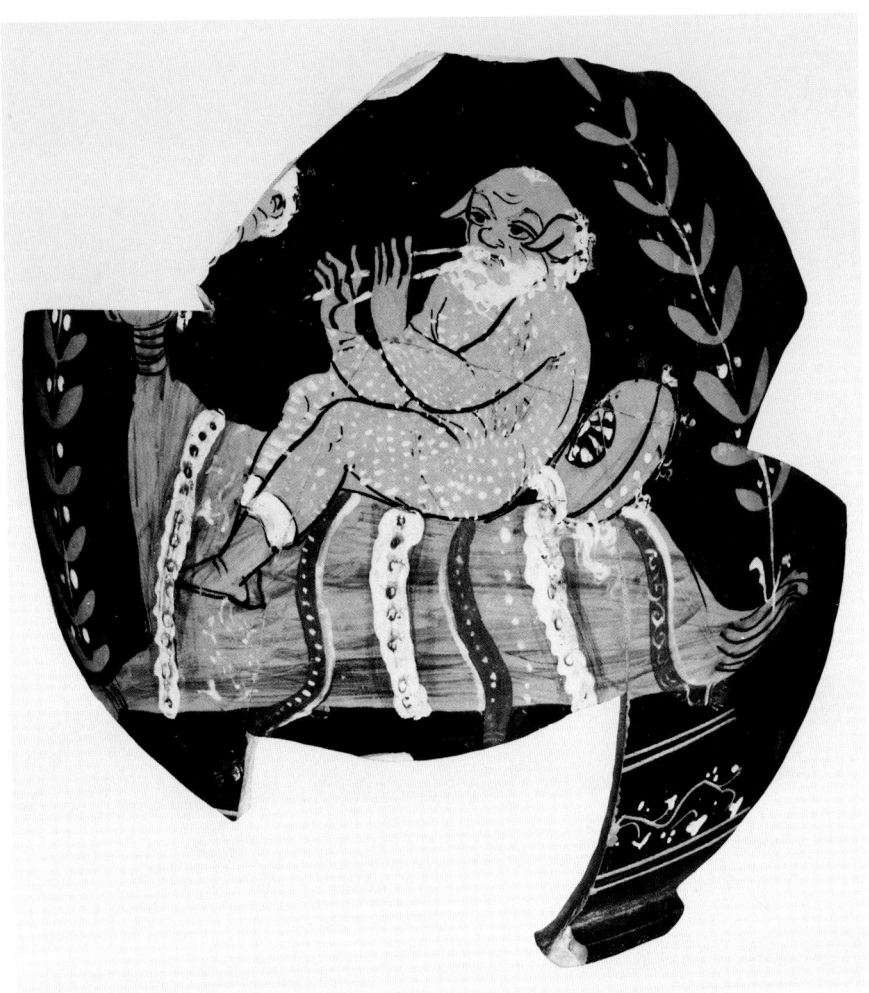

45. Sicilian Squat Lekythos Fragment
Attributed to the Lentini Group
Circa 350-325 B.C.
Height: 13.2 cm.
Checklist no. 205.

On this fragment from an ornate Sicilian squat lekythos, an old Silen reclines on a bloated wineskin, playing the double flutes. The skin is strewn with patterned fillets, alternately red and yellow; and a small round cushion supports the Silen's furry back. In fact the entire body of the Silen, except for hands and feet, is covered with short white hair which matches his full beard. On his feet he wears fur-trimmed boots. A cloudlike form seems to be billowing up from the left end of the skin, and perhaps some part of a floral design remains above the flutist's head. The charming little figure is flanked on either side by upright branches of olive trees with fruits attached, and the groundline beneath is formed by an ivy vine covered with leaves and berries.

A lavish use of colors enlivens the composition, and it is easy to see that the South Italian taste for ornament, even in a fairly simple design, arose from an aesthetic sense quite different from that which inspired Attic vase painters. Yet this rather original treatment of a common Dionysiac subject, the fluting satyr, is perfectly suited in scale and mood to the small vase which it once decorated.

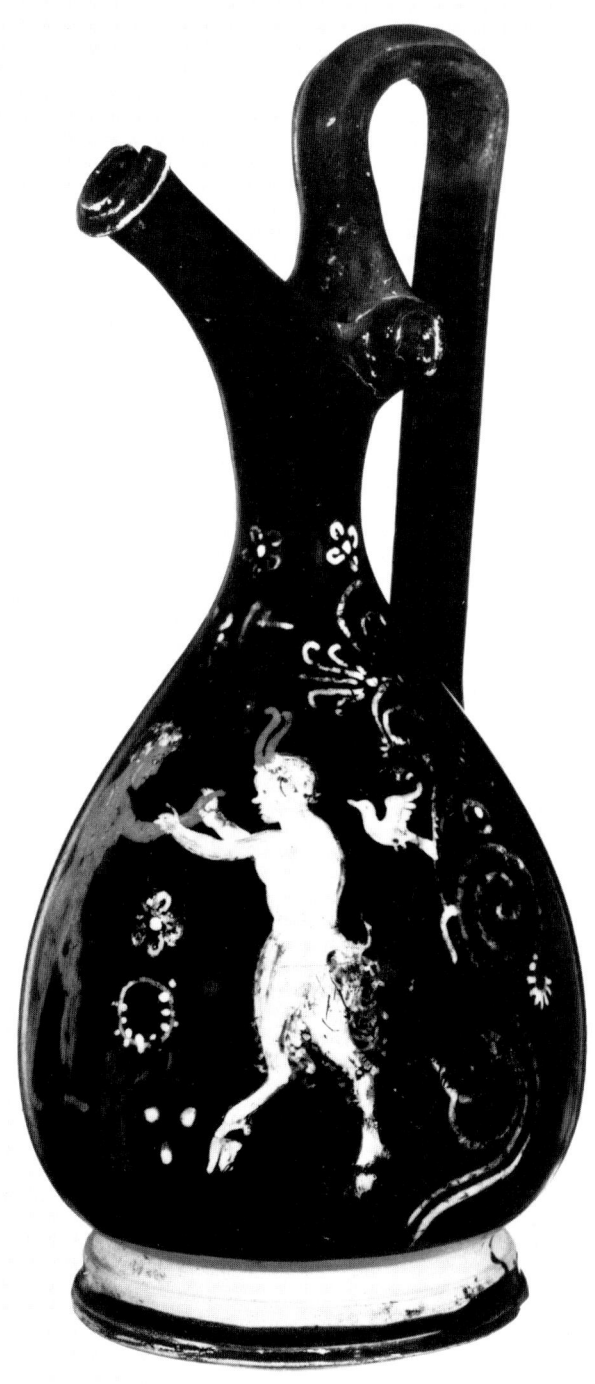

46. Gnathian Oinochoe, Shape 10
Circa 350 B.C.
Height: 18 cm.
Checklist no. 244.

The first impression that this vase gives is one of precious decoration. Only on second glance does one notice the subject, the amorous goat-god Pan wrestling with a nude youth. Between them is a flowered wreath. A white dove flies out from one of the flowering plants that border the scene with a profusion of tendrils, small plastic faces adorn the sides of the handle at the point of attachment to the mouth, and the overall effect is purely ornamental.

Gnathian pottery is named for the ancient site in Apulia where this distinctive ware was found in quantity in the nineteenth century, but its manufacture was not restricted to this site. Unlike the South Italian fabrics which sought to imitate the popular imported Greek red-figure vases, Gnathian ware is usually decorated with floral motives painted on the surface in bright added colors—mostly white, red, and yellow—which contrast with the black glaze background. Figures like the Pan and youth on this vase are rarer and mostly restricted to the earlier years of the technique.

At first, Gnathian decoration was applied to standard red-figure vase shapes, but the technique fairly quickly modified the well-known profiles to shapes better suited to its decorative needs. Being a very ornamental style, Gnathian decoration is most appropriate for small pots, and its vines and figures often recall the Dionysiac revels where vessels such as this little oinochoe would have been used.

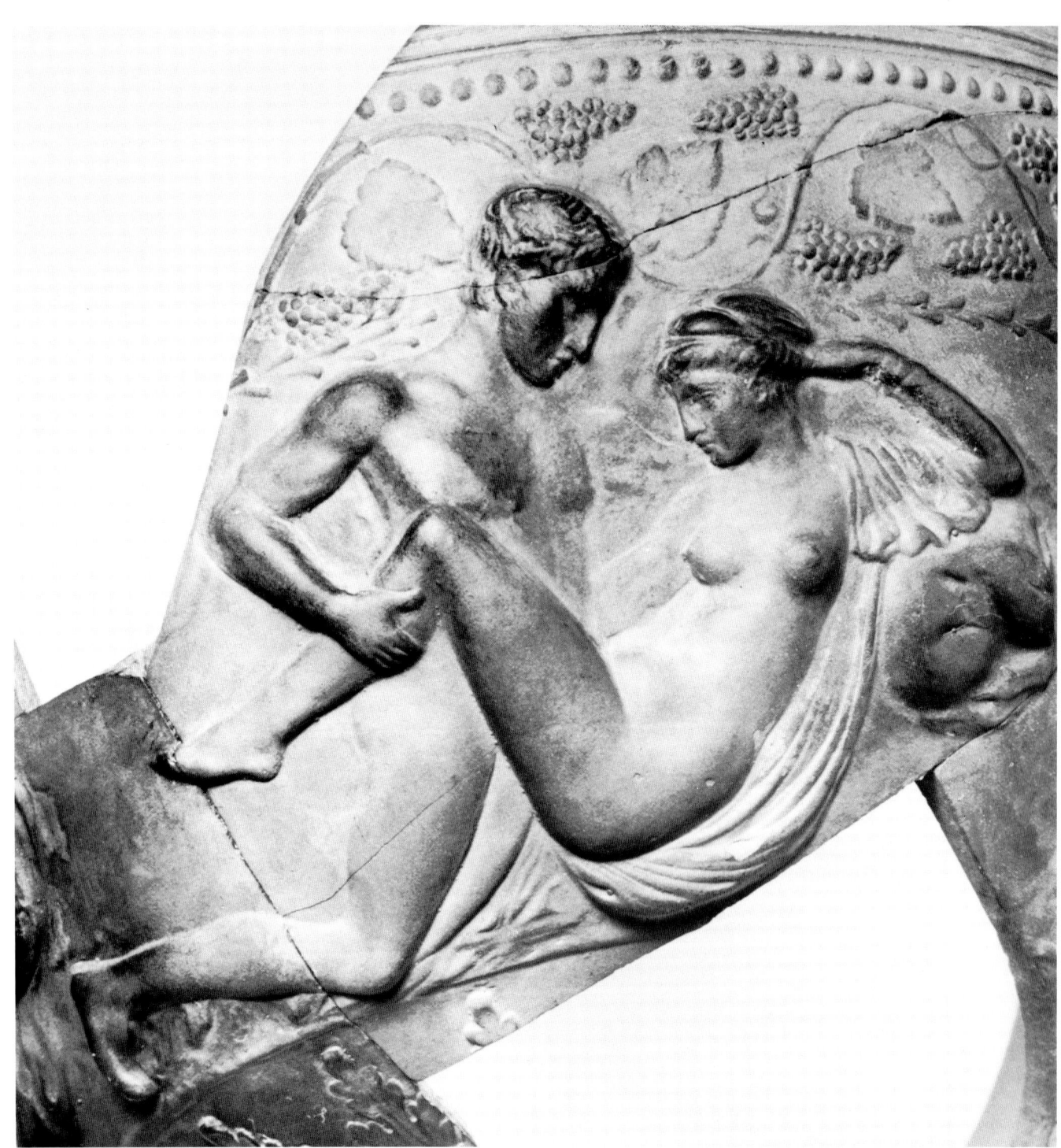

47. Bowl
Stamped with the name PERENNI
Later first century B.C.
Diameter (est): 16.4 cm.
Checklist no. 253.

Three couples (originally there were four) are to be seen on this bowl in low relief, crisp as a freshly-struck medallion. They make an appropriate illustration for the Roman poet Ovidius' *Ars amatoria*. The date is the same, and the intention too, with the difference that the figures here are stylized in the ennobling spirit of Augustan classicism, while Ovidius is more descriptive. The piece bears the stamp of the workshop of Perennius (probably the senior of the two ceramicists bearing this name). Several replicas and variants of the same molded series are known.

In one respect, this bowl is different from the others. As Dietrich von Bothmer pointed out, the vase was not glazed before firing; consequently it lacks the lustrous brick-red finish characteristic of Arretine ware. That is the reason why the contours of the figures are much sharper than usual. The precision of the lines rivals the drawing on Attic white-ground wares of the best kind (compare No. 35). However elevated the style of the representation, though, the sophisticated eroticism is far from the natural spontaneity of similar scenes on Attic vases from the end of the sixth and beginning of the fifth centuries B.C. (compare, for example, the exterior of the cup by Onesimos, No. 37 above). The times have changed, and the mores too.

CHECKLIST OF ANCIENT VASES IN THE COLLECTION OF MOLLY AND WALTER BAREISS

MYCENAEAN

1. Miniature Stirrup Jar
Ca. 1300 B.C.
Floral patterns, dark on light. Top and spout restored.

S.80.AE.38 Bareiss 255

2. Three-handled Alabastron
Ca. 1250 B.C.
Geometric patterns, dark on light.

S.82.AE.53 Bareiss 28

ATTIC GEOMETRIC

3. Trefoil Oinochoe with Female Breasts in High Relief
Ca. 800-750 B.C.

S.80.AE.35 Bareiss 251

4. One-handled Mug
Ca. 750-725 B.C.

S.80.AE.58 Bareiss 428

PROTO-CORINTHIAN AND CORINTHIAN

5. Proto-Corinthian Olpe, Fragmentary
Ca. 630 B.C.
Attributed to the Painter of Vatican 73 [Cahn]
In four registers, Top: Sphinxes and panthers; 2nd: Lions, goat; 3rd: Swan, sphinxes, panther, goat; 4th: Boar, panther, goat, lion, bull.

S.80.AE.328 Bareiss 313

6. Proto-Corinthian Pointed Aryballos
Ca. 650-625 B.C.
Upper register: Confronted sphinxes and grazing goat.
Lower register: Hounds pursuing a hare.
Neck and greatest part of mouth restored.

S.82.AE.1 Bareiss 240

7. Proto-Corinthian Pointed Aryballos
Ca. 650-625 B.C.
On shoulder: Two hounds pursuing a hare.
On body: Three riders galloping to right.
Neck and handle missing.

S.82.AE.12 Bareiss 219

8. Corinthian Column Krater Fragment
Ca. 570-560 B.C.
Upper register: Remains of five pairs of padded dancers, one of whom is a flutist.
Remnants of two registers of animals below.

S.80.AE.126 Bareiss 170

9. Corinthian Alabastron
Early sixth century B.C.
Two confronted cocks.

S.80.AE.31 Bareiss 214

10. Corinthian Aryballos
Ca. 575 B.C.
Crouching lion to right looking back, and a swan.

S.80.AE.32 Bareiss 215

11. Corinthian Alabastron
Ca. 575 B.C.
Confronted lions, with an owl between them.

S.80.AE.323 Bareiss 218

12. Corinthian Alabastron
Ca. 575 B.C.
Attributed to the Panther-bird Painter [Amyx]
Male siren wearing a polos crown; his wings are outspread to right; behind his right wing, a fish.

S.80.AE.69   Bareiss 217

13. Corinthian Lekanis Lid Fragment
Ca. 575 B.C.
Siren to left.

S.80.AE.158   Bareiss 340

CHALCIDIAN

14. Hydria
Ca. 530-520 B.C.
Attributed to the Painter of the Cambridge Hydria [Bothmer]
On the shoulder: Alternating grazing goats and owls three times, with extra owl at right end.
On the body, front: Heraldic panthers between seated sphinxes; back: sirens; under each horizontal handle: Preening swan.

S.82.AE.7   Bareiss 145

14 bis. Amphora
Ca. 520-510 B.C.
Attributed to the Phineus Painter [Bothmer]
A: Rider.
B: Man and woman in conversation.

S.82.AE.15   Bareiss 430

*15. Eye Cup (See No. 3, p. 12, fig. 3.)
Ca. 520 B.C.
Attributed to the Phineus Painter [Bothmer]
A and B: Nose between eyes and ears, with large palmettes at the handles. Compound lotus bud above nose on A; single bud on B.

S.82.AE.16   Bareiss 394

LACONIAN

16. Cup, Fragmentary
Ca. 540 B.C.
Attributed to the Boread Painter [Bothmer]
I: Boreads pursuing Harpies; in the exergue, lion.

S.83.AE.1

*17. Cup (See No. 2, p. 11, fig. 2.)
Ca. 540 B.C.
Attributed to the Hunt Painter [Shefton]
I: Lion with head averted.

S.82.AE.6   Bareiss 317

EUBOEAN

*18. Neck Amphora (See No. 4, pp. 12-13, fig. 4.)
Ca. 570-560 B.C.
By the same hand as S.80.AE.253 (no. 19) [Bothmer]
A: Two draped men in conversation between two sphinxes. In lower register: Palmette-lotus hybrid between two sirens which are flanked by lions with averted heads.
B: The Judgment of Paris. In lower register: A cock between two sirens which are flanked by lions with averted heads.

S.80.AE.303   Bareiss 236

19. Neck Amphora
Ca. 570-560 B.C.
By the same hand as S.80.AE.303 (no. 18) [Bothmer]
A: Herakles battling Kyknos, while Athena and Hermes look on from the left and Ares and Aphrodite look on from the right.
B: Draped man standing between two women, flanked by seated sphinxes. On the neck, A: Confronted lions with dot rosettes between; B: The same lions with palmettes/lotus hybrid replacing the rosettes.
In the register beneath, A: Standing draped youth between seated lions with averted heads, all flanked by sirens; B: Seated lion with head turned, between sirens with wings raised, all flanked by lions.
Etruscan graffito.

S.80.AE.253   Bareiss 237

20. Plate
Ca. 500 B.C.
I: Running Iris or Nike; below her feet, a snake. Ivy wreath around the rim.

S.82.AE.3   Bareiss 239

EAST GREEK

21. Lip Cup
Ca. 540-530 B.C.
I: Concentric circles around the inner bowl; broad circle and dot in the center.

S.82.AE.4   Bareiss 398

*22. Lip Cup (See No. 1, p. 10, fig. 1.)
Ca. 530 B.C.
I: Water fowl in a procession around the inside of the offset lip; star rosette in the tondo.
A and B: Ivy wreath around the lip; palmettes at the handle roots.

S.82.AE.5   Bareiss 208

23. Faience Alabastron
Early sixth century B.C.
Upper register: Herdsman with goats.
Lower register: Herdsman with cattle.

S.82.AE.17   Bareiss 425

24. Faience Aryballos
Early sixth century B.C.
Body decorated with incised net pattern; black lines on the shoulder and around the outer edge of mouth.

S.80.AE.48   Bareiss 354

ATTIC BLACK-FIGURE

*25. Amphora Type A (See No. 5, p. 14, fig. 5.)
Ca. 550-540 B.C.
Attributed to Lydos, or someone close to him [Bothmer]
A: Theseus battling the Minotaur between two groups of onlookers, each group including two men and one woman.
B: Two youths on horseback, with one youth behind them and two women and a man before them.

S.82.AE.38   Bareiss 1

26. Amphora Type A, Fragment
Ca. 530 B.C.
Attributed to the Antimenes Painter [Bothmer]
On rim: Boar and lion twice.

S.80.AE.272   Bareiss 17

27. Amphora Type B
Ca. 540 B.C.
Attributed to the Manner of the Princeton Painter [Beazley]
Potted by Amasis [Bothmer]
A: The recovery of Helen by Menelaus and another warrior.
B: Two hoplites in combat between two men, one of whom is aged.

S.80.AE.296   Bareiss 6

28. Amphora Type B
Ca. 530-520 B.C.
Attributed to the Rycroft Painter [Beazley]
A: Warrior and his charioteer in a quadriga that is beginning to turn.
B: Dionysos mounted on a mule, attended by two satyrs.
Etruscan graffito.

S.82.AE.238   Bareiss 3

29. Amphora Type B
Ca. 530-520 B.C.
Same hand as Florence 3797; both close to the Witt Painter [Bothmer]
A: Seated Herakles between Athena and Hermes (Athena's shield device: sphinx).
B: Athena between Zeus and another god(?) (Athena's shield device: flying bird).

S.80.AE.3   Bareiss 4

30. Amphora Type B (small)
Ca. 530-520 B.C.
Attributed to the Dot-ivy Group [Bothmer]
A: Duel between two hoplites flanked by two draped youths (shield device of right hoplite: chariot box).
B: Warrior between two draped youths who hold upright spears (shield device of warrior: three balls).

S.80.AE.182

*31. Amphora Type C (See No. 6, p. 15, fig. 6.)
Ca. 530 B.C.
Attributed to the Affecter Painter [Beazley]
Potted by the same artist.
A: Two nude men between two draped observers.
B: Three nude men dancing around a man dressed in a long chiton and himation.
Etruscan graffito.

S.80.AE.241   Bareiss 21

32. Small Panathenaic Amphora
Ca. 540-530 B.C.
Attributed to the Swing Painter [Bothmer]
A: Athena to the left between two columns surmounted by cocks (shield device: tripod).
B: Two wrestlers flanked by judges; between the wrestlers, a dinos (prize).

S.80.AE.82   Bareiss 367

33. Neck Amphora (Ovoid)
Ca. 570-560 B.C.
On neck, A and B: Panther leaping to the right.
On the black body: Three pairs of red stripes.

S.80.AE.234   Bareiss 315

34. Neck Amphora
Ca. 550 B.C.
On neck, A and B: Head of a bearded man.
A and B, in panels: Each, youth on horseback galloping to the right.

S.80.AE.26   Bareiss 133

35. Neck Amphora
Ca. 540 B.C.
Attributed to the Circle of Group E, Painter of London B 174 [Bothmer]
On shoulder, A: Cavalcade of four riders with a draped youth standing at the rear; B: Cavalcade of four riders.
On body, A: Battle scenes: three duels, two over a fallen warrior; B: Three hoplites between two mounted youths (horses frontal), a draped man and youth, and two nude youths.
Shield devices: lion protome, four stars around central ball, swan, star, plane leaf.
Etruscan graffito.
Ancient repairs.

S.80.AE.41   Bareiss 262

36. Neck Amphora, Fragmentary
Ca. 540 B.C.
Attributed to the Painter of the Nicosia Olpe [Bothmer]
A: Theseus and the Minotaur.
B: Arming scene.
Palmette-lotus chain below the figured scenes.

S.80.AE.224   Bareiss 364

*37. Neck Amphora (See No. 7, p. 16, fig. 7.)
Ca. 530 B.C.
Attributed to the Affecter Painter [Beazley]
Potted by the same artist
On the neck, A and B: Three dancing men.
A: Herakles battling the centaur Nessos in the center of a group of four men, one with head averted toward side B.
B: Theseus in combat with the Minotaur; three men look on and one other runs away with head turned back toward Side A.
Etruscan graffito.

S.82.AE.47   Bareiss 20

38. Neck Amphora
Ca. 530 B.C.
Attributed to the Three Line Group, same hand as Berlin 1841 [Beazley]
A: Herakles struggling with the Nemean lion between Athena and Iolaos.
B: Herakles and Athena, Dionysos and Ariadne (or perhaps Semele).
Inscribed: ΚΑΛΙΑΣ ΚΑΛΟΣ
Much missing.

S.80.AE.5   Bareiss 13

*39. Neck Amphora (See No. 8, p. 18, fig. 8.)
Ca. 530 B.C.
Assigned to the Class of Neck Amphorae with Shoulder Pictures [Bothmer]
On the shoulders in panels,
A: Running Gorgon between eyes;
B: Running Iris between eyes.
Etruscan graffito.

S.80.AE.228   Bareiss 10

40. Neck Amphora (White-ground)
Ca. 520 B.C.
Attributed to the Group of Faina 75 [Cahn]
A: Combat between two hoplites, one of whom has fallen.
B: The like.

S.80.AE.2

41. Neck Amphora
Ca. 520-510 B.C.
A: Dionysos standing to right, looking back, with a goat beside him, a fluting satyr on the left, and a dancing maenad on the right.
B: Two men leading horses.

S.80.AE.66   Bareiss 144

42. Neck Amphora
Ca. 520-510 B.C.
Attributed to the Leagros Group [Bothmer]
A: Herakles, accompanied by Athena and Hermes, capturing Kerberos.
B: Dionysos and a maenad between two satyrs.

S.80.AE.230   Bareiss 12

43. Neck Amphora
Ca. 520-510 B.C.
Attributed to the Leagros Group [Bothmer]
A: Achilleus and Aias gaming, with the goddess Athena standing between them (shield devices: Achilleus, tripod; Aias, bull's head).
B: Three hoplites standing facing left (shield devices: left to right, three balls, the letter N, a drinking horn).

S.80.AE.292   Bareiss 9

44. Neck Amphora
Ca. 520-510 B.C.
Attributed to the Leagros Group [Bothmer]
On neck, A: Quadriga; B: Departure of a warrior; unmeaning inscriptions on both sides.
A: Aineas rescuing his father Anchises, with his son Askanios leading the way and Aphrodite looking on from behind.
Inscribed: ΓΕΤΕΛΕΥΧ (unmeaning)
ΑΦΡΟΔΙΤΕ ΚΑΛΕ
ΑΝΗΡΙ (retrograde)
ΑΙΝΕΑ : ΚΑΛΟΣ
B: Dionysos between satyr flutist and satyr.
S.82.AE.48   Bareiss 352

45. Neck Amphora
Ca. 520-510 B.C.
Attributed to the Leagros Group [Bothmer]
A: Herakles threatening Eurystheus with the Erymanthian boar, while Athena and another woman look on.
B: Farewell scene, with a warrior and his dog between an old man and woman (shield device: running dog).
S.80.AE.232   Bareiss 143

46. Neck Amphora
Ca. 520-510 B.C.
Attributed to the Leagros Group, Side B near the Acheloos Painter [Beazley]
A: Two satyrs carrying off a pair of maenads.
B: Four dancing revelers.
S.80.AE.4   Bareiss 11

*47. Neck Amphora (See No. 10, pp. 20-21, figs. 10a-b.)
Ca. 520-510 B.C.
Attributed to the Medea Group, Bareiss Painter (name piece) [Bothmer]
A: The apotheosis of Herakles.
B: Two mounted warriors in combat over a fallen hoplite.
The mouth was evidently broken in antiquity and replaced with the mouth of an amphora of the same size with similar decoration but made some ten to fifteen years later [Bothmer].
S.82.AE.2   Bareiss 14

48. Neck Amphora
Ca. 480-450 B.C.
Attributed to the Group of Würzburg 221 (by the same hand as the name piece) [Bothmer]
A: Herakles and the centaur Pholos.
B: Two centaurs carrying branches. Stripes around the lower body.
S.80.AE.65   Bareiss 134

49. Neck Amphora Fragments, Nicosthenic Shape
Ca. 530 B.C.
Attributed to Painter N, belonging to his Thiasos Group [Beazley]
Signed: ΝΙΚΟΣΘΕΝΕΙΣ ΕΓΟΙΕΣΕΝ
On each handle: Dancing satyr.
On the shoulder, A: Mounted youth to left beween two nude youths and two draped men; B: At least two running figures and two horses.
Below a band of ribbon pattern on A and B, dancing maenads and satyrs.
S.80.AE.85   Bareiss 16

50. Neck Amphora Fragments, Nicosthenic Shape
Ca. 550-540 B.C.
Attributed to Painter N, belonging to his Overlap Group [Bothmer]
In overlap decoration on the body: Remains of six warriors in combat (shield devices: snakes, rays).
S.80.AE.50   Bareiss 365

51. Neck Amphora Lid
Second half of the sixth century B.C.
Black stripes with dotted band at the outer edge.
S.80.AE.142   Bareiss 203

52. Amphora Lid
Second half of the sixth century B.C.
Striped, with ivy wreath around the outer edge.
S.80.AE.184   Bareiss 262a

53. Stamnos
Ca. 500 B.C.
Attributed to the Beaune Painter [Bothmer]
A and B, within panels, in two registers: Men and women banqueting.
Dipinti on bottom: ΣΟ
S.80.AE.320   Bareiss 318

54. Volute Krater Fragment
Ca. 530 B.C.
On the rim: A boar to right, a bull to left.
S.80.AE.8   Bareiss 37

55. Volute Krater Fragment
Ca. 530-520 B.C.
On the neck: A figure in a himation before a wheeling quadriga.
S.80.AE.25   Bareiss 129

56. Volute Krater Fragments (Four)
Ca. 520-510 B.C.
On the neck: The departure of warriors in quadrigas, hoplites, archers, Hermes, seated man to right (shield devices: snakes and rosette).

S.80.AE.11.1-4   Bareiss 41a-d

57. Volute Krater Fragment
Ca. 520-510 B.C.
Attributed to the Golvol Group [Bothmer]
On the neck, from left to right, between sphinxes and eyes: seated man in a dotted himation, and a quadriga to right with the charioteer prepared for departure.

S.80.AE.10   Bareiss 40

58. Column Krater, Fragmentary
Ca. 560 B.C.
Attributed to the Fallow Deer Painter of the Tyrrhenian Group [Bothmer]
A: Warriors dueling while their mothers look on (Achilleus and Memnon?).
B: Six komasts.
Under the handle: Eyes.
Unmeaning inscriptions.

S.80.AE.176   Bareiss 325

59. Hydria
Ca. 550 B.C.
Attributed to the Wider Circle of Lydos [Cahn]
On the shoulder: Four warriors in combat over the body of a fifth (shield devices: flying bird, cock).
On the body: Dionysos and goddess facing Poseidon.

S.82.AE.45

*60. Hydria (See No. 9, p. 19, fig. 9.)
Ca. 510 B.C.
Attributed to the Lykomedes Painter [Bothmer]
On the shoulder: Herakles wrestling the Nemean lion.
On the body: Apollo struggling with Herakles for the Delphic tripod, as Artemis and Athena look on.
Inscribed: ΛΑ+ΕΜΙΔΕϟ (= Artemidos)
ΑΠΟ[ΛΟ]ΝΟS (retrograde)
ΗΕΡΑΚΛΕΟS
Α]ΘΕΝΑS
The edges of the foot and mouth are painted white.

S.82.AE.33   Bareiss 23

61. Hydria
Ca. 510 B.C.
Attributed to the Leagros Group, same hand as *ABV* 365, 71 [Bothmer]
On the shoulder: Quadriga race.
On the body: Dionysos, holding a kantharos and grapevine, seated among four dancing maenads.

S.80.AE.181   Bareiss 139

62. Kalpis
Ca. 510 B.C.
By the same hand as Würzburg 323 [Bothmer], which Langlotz compared with a kalpis attributed by Beazley to the Manner of the Acheloos Painter Departure of a hoplite and a Scythian archer in a quadriga; before them, an old man.

S.80.AE.250   Bareiss 25

63. Kalpis Fragment
Ca. 510 B.C.
In a panel: Apollo seated to right before a low altar and playing the kithara for Leto on the left and Artemis on the right.
Inscribed: ΛΕΤΟ
ΑΠΟΛΟΝ
ΑΡΤΕΜΙS
In the handle zone: Running horizontal palmettes in tendrils.
For the scheme of decoration, compare Leningrad 5571 [Bothmer].

S.80.AE.174   Bareiss A16

64. Olpe
Ca. 500 B.C.
Aineas carrying his father Anchises from Troy, with a young Scythian archer (Askanios?) behind and a woman (Kreusa?) and an old man before him.

S.80.AE.294   Bareiss 233

65. Olpe
Ca. 490 B.C.
Attributed to the Dot-ivy Group [Bothmer]
Athena Polias between two columns surmounted by cocks; on the tendril behind the goddess' heel, an owl (shield device: tripod, with plastic snake head protruding).
The subject imitates Side A of Panathenaic amphorae except that the Athena is turned in the opposite direction.

S.80.AE.70   Bareiss 232

66. Trefoil Oinochoe, Shape 2
Ca. 520-510 B.C.
For the rays on the collar, compare with oinochoai of the Guide-line Class [Beazley]
Aias and another warrior pursuing Kassandra toward the Palladion (shield devices: Aias, white and red circles; right warrior, ivy wreath).

S.80.AE.293   Bareiss 98

67. Trefoil Oinochoe, Shape 1
Ca. 520-510 B.C.
Assigned to the Keyside Class [Bothmer]
Peleus and Thetis.

S.80.AE.297   Bareiss 97

68. Oinochoe Fragment
Ca. 520-510 B.C.
Assigned to the Class of Vatican G.47 [Bothmer]
Wheeling quadriga team to right, with a warrior to left at the far side of the left trace horse.

S.80.AE.179   Bareiss 100

69. Trefoil Oinochoe, Shape 1
Ca. 510-500 B.C.
Attributed to the Painter of Oxford 225 [Beazley]
Maenad riding a bull.

S.80.AE.302   Bareiss 96

70. Lekythos
Ca. 530 B.C.
Attributed to Phanyllis Group, B, the Group of the Arming Lekythoi [Bothmer]
On shoulder: Two draped youths flanking a central palmette.
On body: Dionysos between two dancing satyrs.

S.80.AE.183   Bareiss 109

71. Lekythos
Ca. 500 B.C.
Attributed to the Gela Painter [Bothmer]
Two centaurs dipping wine from a sunken pithos in the cave of Pholos; between them, a kantharos.
On the shoulder: Three palmettes, two buds.
The foot is restored.

S.80.AE.19   Bareiss 107

72. Lekythos
Ca. 500 B.C.
Attributed to the Leagros Group
Potted by the same hand as New York 56.171.33 [Bothmer]
Dionysos holding a drinking horn between two maenads mounted on ithyphallic mules.

S.80.AE.227   Bareiss 341

73. Lekythos
Ca. 500-490 B.C.
Assigned to the Little Lion Class, Krotala Group [Bothmer]
On the shoulder: Two lions.
On the body: Athena in combat with a giant between two onlookers who hold spears.

S.80.AE.326   Bareiss 110

74. Epinetron Fragment
Ca. 520-510 B.C.
Attributed to the Sappho Painter [Bothmer]
On the upper surface: Incised scale patterns.
On the side: Quadriga team to right. Around the curved surface of the front: Rays.

S.80.AE.112   Bareiss 152

*75. Nicosthenic Pyxis Fragment
(See No. 15, p. 27, fig. 15.)
Ca. 540 B.C.
Attributed to the BMN Painter [Bothmer]
Gigantomachy: Athena in a quadriga, Herakles behind, doing battle with Porphyrios and Enkelados.
Inscribed: ΑΘENA
ΦΟΡΦΥΡΙΟΝ retrograde
ΕΝΚΕΛΑΔΟΣ retrograde

S.82.AE.26   Bareiss 351

76. Tripod Pyxis
Ca. 540 B.C.
On lid: Athletes (boxers, wrestlers, and discus thrower) and referees.
On legs, A: Herakles and the lion; B: Courting scene (man and youth between komasts); C: Theseus and the Minotaur.

S.80.AE.322   Bareiss 433

77. Kyathos
Ca. 520-510 B.C.
Satyr pursuing a maenad between eyes. Dancing youths on either side of the handle, which is restored.

S.80.AE.73   Bareiss 345

78. Kyathos
Ca. 520-510 B.C.
Related to the group of Vatican 480 [Bothmer]
Two lions attacking a bull in the midst of five men and youths.

S.80.AE.80   Bareiss 122

*79. Kyathos (White-ground)
(See No. 16, pp. 28-29, fig. 16.)
Ca. 510 B.C.
Attributed to a follower of the Theseus Painter [Eisman]
Perseus pursuing the running Gorgons.

S.82.AE.40   Bareiss 124

80. Kyathos
Ca. 500-490 B.C.
Attributed to the Theseus Painter [Bothmer]
Reclining Herakles, a maenad, and three satyrs, one dancing, one carrying a wineskin, and one carrying a pointed amphora.

S.82.AE.41   Bareiss 123

80 *bis*. Black Glazed Skyphos
Ca. 540 B.C.

S.82.AE.39   Bareiss 355

81. Skyphos
Ca. 540-530 B.C.
Attributed to the Camel Painter [Bothmer]
A and B: Two warriors in combat between youths in himatia (shield device of left hoplite on each side: projecting snake protome).

S.80.AE.296   Bareiss 43

82. Mastoid Cup
Ca. 510-500 B.C.
Herakles reclining between Iolaos and Athena, who are seated on blocks, while Hermes dips wine from a large column krater.
Much missing.

S.80.AE.24   Bareiss 125

*83. Siana Cup (Overlap)
(See No. 11, pp. 22-23, figs. 11a-b.)
Ca. 580-570 B.C.
I: Rider.
A: Calydonian Boar Hunt.
B: Battle between the centaurs and the Lapiths, with Kaineus in the center being pounded into the ground with stones by two centaurs (shield device: tripod).
Unmeaning inscription.

S.82.AE.46   Bareiss 248

84. Siana Cup, Fragmentary (Double-decker)
Ca. 570 B.C.
Attributed to the Heidelberg Painter [Beazley]
I: Warrior putting on greaves.
A and B: Battle scenes, with chariot on A and fallen warrior under the preserved handle.
On the rim: Lotus bud festoon.

S.80.AE.16   Bareiss 94

85. Siana Cup (Overlap; two fragments from many)
Ca. 570-560 B.C.
Attributed to the BMN Painter [Beazley]
I: Swan.
A: Calydonian Boar Hunt.
B: Wounded stag between two mounted riders.
Unmeaning inscriptions.

S.80.AE.17.1 and 2   Bareiss 95

*86. Lip Cup (See No. 12, p. 24, fig. 12.)
Ca. 550-540 B.C.
Signed by Epitimos as potter,
A: E[ΠIT]IM[OS EΠ]OIESEN
B: EΠITIMOS EΠOI]ESE[N
I: Standing figure, seated Zeus, Hermes, and seated goddess (Hera?); in exergue, confronted cocks.
A: On lip, rider to right; in handle zone, sphinxes.
B: The like.
Burned in antiquity; now refired.

S.80.AE.40   Bareiss 395

87. Lip Cup
Ca. 540 B.C.
I: Winged youth running to the right.
A and B: Each, signed by Sokles as potter,
A: SOKLES [EΠ]OI[E]SEN
B: SOKLES EΠOIESEN

S.80.AE.255   Bareiss 393

*88. Lip Cup (See No. 13, pp. 24-25, fig. 13.)
Ca. 540 B.C.
Attributed to the Tleson Painter [Bothmer]
A and B: A cock to left, in a position of attack.
Repaired in antiquity.

S.80.AE.60   Bareiss 90

89. Lip Cup
Ca. 540 B.C.
A and B: Confronted rams.
In each handle zone (worn on one side), inscribed:
A: +AIPE KAI ΠIEITENΔE
B: +AIRE KAI ΠIEITEN[Δ]E
("Hail and drink this").

S.80.AE.68   Bareiss 209

90. Lip Cup
Ca. 540 B.C.
I: Lion attacking a bull.
The foot, stem, and one handle are restored.

S.80.AE.249   Bareiss 141

91. Lip Cup
Ca. 540 B.C.
May be by the Elbows Out Painter [Bothmer]
I: Dancing youth and bearded reveler.

S.80.AE.298   Bareiss 91

92. Lip Cup
Ca. 530 B.C.
A: Rider between two running youths.
B: Rider following a walking youth.
Unmeaning inscriptions.

S.80.AE.61   Bareiss 92

93. Cup Type A (Lipped inside)
Ca. 530 B.C.
Attributed to Nikosthenes as potter [Bothmer]
I: Running Iris.
A: Athena battling two giants, who crouch behind the apotropaic eyes.
B: Athena in combat with a single giant.
Around each handle: Herakles in combat with a giant; under each handle: a child (A/B, youth; B/A, girl).

S.80.AE.229   Bareiss 83

94. Cup Type A (See No. 14, pp. 26-27, fig. 14.)
Ca. 530 B.C.
Compared by Beazley with the cup Vatican 456
Signed by Nikosthenes as potter:
    NIKOSΘENES EΠOIESEN
A: Between eyes, busts of Herakles and Athena.
B: Between eyes, busts of a man and two women, one of whom wears a polos crown (Hades, Demeter, and Persephone? [Bothmer])
Beneath handle A/B: Rooster.
Beneath handle B/A: Boar.
The foot and stem are restored.

S.80.AE.300   Bareiss 82

95. Segment Cup Fragment
Ca. 510-500 B.C.
I: Man dressed in himation, seated to right beside a kitharist standing to right dressed in chiton and himation (Herakles and Apollo?).

S.80.AE.96   Bareiss 73

*96. Exaleiptron (See No. 17, p. 29, fig. 17.)
Ca. 500 B.C.
Bands of alternating red and black tongues and dots.

S.82.AE.59   Bareiss 454

ATTIC RED-FIGURE

*97. Neck Amphora with Double Handles (See No. 21, pp. 32-35, figs. 21a-c.)   Ca. 480 B.C.
Attributed to the Berlin Painter [Beazley]
A: Dancing youth holding a kylix in one hand.
B: Dancing man; his features are those of a non-Greek.
Etruscan graffito.

S.80.AE.327   Bareiss 15

98. Nolan Amphora
Ca. 440 B.C.
Attributed to the Richmond Painter [Beazley]
A: Nike.
B: Draped youth with a walking stick.

S.80.AE.247   Bareiss 135

99. Nolan Amphora
Ca. 440 B.C.
Attributed to the Richmond Painter [Beazley]
A: Draped satyr pursuing a youth.
B: Draped youth.
Etruscan graffito.

S.80.AE.246   Bareiss 136

100. Pelike
Ca. 470 B.C.
Attributed to the Triptolemos Painter [Beazley]
A: Theseus and Aigeus(?) with Poseidon.
B: Man offering a hare as a love gift to a youth.

S.80.AE.235   Bareiss 347

101. Pelike, Kerch style
Ca. 380 B.C.
Attributed to the Painter of Munich 2365 [Bothmer]
A: Three Arimasps battling griffins.
B: Three draped youths conversing.

S.80.AE.301   Bareiss 22

102. Column Krater
Ca. 480 B.C.
Attributed to Myson [Beazley]
A: Athletes training (left to right, acontist, trainer, and jumper practicing with weights).
B: Two youths with horses.
On the rim, A: Grazing deer and panthers in silhouette; B: Grazing goats and panthers in silhouette.

S.80.AE.231   Bareiss 432

103. Column Krater
Ca. 480-470 B.C.
Attributed to the Tyszkiewicz Painter [Beazley]
A: Zeus pursuing a woman; another woman running away.
B: Satyr pursuing a maenad.
The foot is modern.

S.80.AE.6   Bareiss 31

104. Column Krater Fragment
Ca. 460 B.C.
A: Bearded god pursuing a female.

S.80.AE.167   Bareiss 253

*105. Calyx Krater Fragment
(See No. 20, p. 00, fig. 20.)
Ca. 520 B.C.
Attributed to Smikros [Beazley]
A: Head of a satyr to left who holds a drinking horn.

S.80.AE.273   Bareiss 34

106. Calyx Krater Fragment
Ca. 430 B.C.
Two Zones, above: Sacrifice of a ram, fight; below: Two young warriors lifting the body of a fallen one; on the right, a grieving warrior who carries three spears and a shield (two of the spears belong to those who carry the dead warrior).

S.80.AE.329   Bareiss 407

107. Calyx Krater Fragment
Ca. 400 B.C.
Originally in two registers, upper: Satyr to right, carrying a plate of food toward a maenad and an animal(?); nothing remains of the bottom register.

S.80.AE.121   Bareiss 162

108. Calyx Krater Fragment
Ca. 380 B.C.
A: Pan peering out to right at a maenad carrying a torch.

S.80.AE.265   Bareiss 186

109. Bell Krater Fragment
Ca. 470 B.C.
Attributed to the Altamura Painter [Bothmer]
A: Head of an old man to left, with his hand raised to hold the crook of his staff.

S.80.AE.274   Bareiss 311

110. Bell Krater Fragment
Ca. 440 B.C.
Attributed to the Circle of Polygnotos [Bothmer]
A: Youths on horseback to right (Dioskouroi?).

S.80.AE.288   Bareiss 1A

*111. Hydria Fragment
(Black-figure shape)
(See No. 19, p. 00, fig. 19.)
Ca. 520 B.C.
Attributed to the Pioneer Group [Beazley]
On the shoulder: Quadriga race to right.
Unmeaning inscription.

S.80.AE.270   Bareiss 24

*112. Kalpis (See No. 24, p. 38, fig. 24.)
Ca. 480 B.C.
Attributed to the Eucharides Painter [Beazley]
Boy playing the double flutes for a youthful reveler.
Inscribed: ΚΑΛΟΣ
ΕΥΧΑΡΙΔΕΣ (retrograde)
One side handle restored.

S.82.AE.42   Bareiss 28

113. Kalpis Fragment
Ca. 480-470 B.C.
Attributed to the Eucharides Painter [Bothmer]
Male figure with a dog.

S.83.AE.12   Bareiss 250

*114. Kalpis Fragment (See No. 22, pp. 32, 36, fig. 22.)
Ca. 480-470 B.C.
Attributed to the Berlin Painter [Bothmer]
Athena and a youth dressed in traveling clothes, holding spears.

S.80.AE.185   Bareiss 29

*115. Kalpis (See No. 25, pp. 38-39, fig. 25, colorpl. p. 9.)
Ca. 480-470 B.C.
Assigned to the Group of the Floral Nolans [Bothmer]
Owl between olive branches.

S.82.AE.43   Bareiss 26

*116. Kalpis (See No. 23, p. 37, fig. 23.)
Ca. 470 B.C.
Attributed as probably by the Aegisthus Painter [Beazley]
Herakles wrestling the Nemean lion.

S.80.AE.233   Bareiss 27

117. Kalpis Fragment
Ca. 440 B.C.
Attributed to the Circle of Polygnotos, probably the Hector Painter [Bothmer]
Thetis and the other nereids bringing the armor to Achilleus, who sits in his tent.

S.82.AE.50   Bareiss 392

*118. Trefoil Oinochoe, Shape 1
(See No. 40, p. 56, fig. 40.)
Ca. 440 B.C.
Attributed to the Richmond Painter [Beazley]
Apollo and Artemis sacrificing over an altar.
Inscribed: ΚΑΛΟΣ ΚΑΛΕ

S.80.AE.258   Bareiss 140

*119. Oinochoe, Shape 3 (Chous)
(See No. 38, p. 54, fig. 38.)
Ca. 470 B.C.
Drunken singing reveler and his young attendant.

S.82.AE.30   Bareiss 101

120. Oinochoe, Shape 4
Late fifth-early fourth century B.C.
Three women: one playing the lyre, one playing the double flutes and beating time with her right foot, and one carrying a chest on her head and a tympanum in her hand.

S.80.AE.244   Bareiss 102

121. Oinochoe, Shape 5A
Ca. 450 B.C.
A: Athlete practicing with jumping weights.
B: Trainer.

S.82.AE.21   Bareiss 434

122. Oinochoe, Shape 8 (Mug, but with two disparate handles)
Ca. 470 B.C.
A: Athlete with a strigil standing by a stool holding folded clothes.
B: Athlete with a strigil standing beside a half column; aryballos and sponge hang behind him.
Inscribed on both sides: ΚΑΛΟΣ

S.82.AE.29   Bareiss 126

*123. Oinochoe, Shape 8C
(See No. 42, pp. 58-59, fig. 42.)
Ca. 430-420 B.C.
Attributed to the Eretria Painter [Beazley]
Squatting boy on see-saw.

S.80.AE.306   Bareiss 103

124. Oinochoe, Fragmentary
Ca. 450 B.C.
Attributed to the Painter of the Berlin Hydria [Beazley]
Dionysos between two maenads, one of whom pours a libation.

S.80.AE.217   Bareiss 138
(augmented with Astarita 796 by Bothmer)

125. Lekythos (White-ground)
Ca. 470-460 B.C.
Attributed to the Bowdoin Painter [Beazley]
Iris pouring a libation from an oinochoe onto a mound-altar.
Unmeaning inscription.

S.80.AE.18   Bareiss 104

126. Lekythos
Ca. 450-440 B.C.
Attributed to the Circle of the Phiale Painter [Cahn]
Nude girl (in added white) holding a mirror, between a chest and a kalathos.

S.80.AE.307   Bareiss 338

127. Lekythos (Black Body)
Ca. 450 B.C.
On shoulder: Four palmettes in silhouette.

S.80.AE.226   Bareiss 108

128. Lekythos (White-ground)
Ca. 450-440 B.C.
Woman dressed in chiton and himation holding a tendril.

S.80.AE.22   Bareiss 118

129. Lekythos (White-ground)
Ca. 440-430 B.C.
Attributed to the Painter of Athens 1826 [Beazley]
A youth tying a fillet around a grave stele as a female servant holding an alabastron looks on. The tomb is seen in rear view, with the tymbos in front of the stele.

S.80.AE.257   Bareiss 105

130. Lekythos
Late fifth century B.C.
Attributed to the Painter of London E 614 [Cook]
Goat to left.

S.80.AE.20   Bareiss 116

131. Lekythos
Late fifth century B.C.
Attributed to the LM Painter [Cook]
Spotted feline (leopard?) leaping to right.

S.80.AE.21   Bareiss 117

132. Lekythos (White-ground)
Ca. 420-410 B.C.
Attributed to the Reed Painter [Beazley]
Youth and maiden on either side of a grave stele within a funerary plot.

S.82.AE.51   Bareiss 429

*133. Squat Lekythos (See No. 41, pp. 57-59, fig. 41.)
Ca. 430-420 B.C.
Attributed to the Eretria Painter [Bothmer]
Satyr playing before a seated sphinx.

S.80.AE.34   Bareiss 244

134. Squat Lekythos
Ca. 410-400 B.C.
Leaping fallow deer.

S.80.AE.63   Bareiss 114

135. Squat Lekythos
Ca. 400 B.C.
Manner of the Meidias Painter [Bothmer]
Eros helping Helen, while Hermes and Paris look on.

S.80.AE.254   Bareiss 300

136. Squat Lekythos
Fourth century B.C.
Assigned to the Bulas Group [Bothmer]
Net pattern with white dots.

S.80.AE.123   Bareiss 167

137. Skyphos Fragment
Ca. 470-460 B.C.
Attributed to the Penthesilea Painter [Cambitoglou]
A: Maenad with thyrsos to right.

S.80.AE.105   Bareiss 120

*138. Skyphos (See No. 39, p. 55, figs. 39a-b.)
Ca. 470-460 B.C.
A: Servant girl balancing a wineskin on her head and carrying a bowl on her back and a jug in her right hand as she walks behind her mistress who is drinking from a huge skyphos.
B: Still life of the interior of a cellar, showing a skyphos, a stand with ladles and an oinochoe suspended, a bronze bail amphora, a hamper, a pointed amphora, and other vessels.

S.80.AE.304   Bareiss 337

139. Skyphos
Ca. 460-450 B.C.
A: Dionysos, with snakes.
B: Giant attacked by a snake of Dionysos (shield device: snake).

S.80.AE.308   Bareiss 348

140. Skyphos Fragment (Corinthian shape)
Ca. 410-400 B.C.
Attributed to the Meidias Painter [Bothmer]
A: Standing woman with head turned to left, holding a large basket in her hand.
By the handles: Florals.

S.80.AE.23   Bareiss 121

141. Kantharoid Skyphos (Handles in the form of Herakles' knots)
Ca. 410 B.C.
Attributed to Aison [Bothmer]
A: Athlete and Eros.
B: Two athletes with javelins.

S.82.AE.44   Bareiss 43

*142. Cup Type A (See No. 18, p. 30, fig. 18.)
Ca. 520 B.C.
Attributed to Psiax [Bothmer]
I: Courting scene (youth and male companion).
A and B: Symposion, with men, youths, and women.
Burned grey in antiquity; refired. Much is missing.

S.82.AE.24   Bareiss 260

*143. Cup Type A (Bilingual) (See No. 26, pp. 40-42, fig. 26.)
Ca. 520 B.C.
Attributed to Oltos [Beazley]
Potted by Hischylos [Bothmer]
I: Running bearded man (black-figure).
Inscribed: MEMNON KALO[S
A: Between eyes, running youth wearing a wreath.
B: Between eyes, nose.
At the handles: Closed palmettes.

S.82.AE.49   Bareiss 81

*144. Cup Type A (See No. 27, pp. 40-42, figs. 27a-b.)
Ca. 510 B.C.
Attributed to Oltos [Beazley]
I: Running satyr carrying a wineskin.

S.82.AE.18   Bareiss 44

*145. Cup Type B (Lipped inside) (See No. 29, p. 43, fig. 29)
Ca. 510 B.C.
Attributed to Epiktetos [Deppert]
I: Reclining reveler, singing and playing the barbitos.
Inscribed: EVOIEOSEN
(misspelled EPOIESEN)

S.80.AE.252   Bareiss 142

146. Cup Type B
Ca. 510-500 B.C.
Attributed to the Ambrosios Painter [Bothmer]
I: Dancing reveler. The interior of the bowl around the tondo is coral red.
Inscribed: ΚΑΛΟS ΝΑ[Ι]+Ι
A and B: Revelers.

S.82.AE.34   Bareiss 242

147. Cup Type B
Ca. 510-500 B.C.
Attributed to the Manner of the Epeleios Painter [Beazley]
I: Youth running with two swords, one of which is unsheathed.
Inscribed: ΚΑΛΟS ΗΟ ΓΑΙS
A and B, each: Boy leading two horses.
Inscribed: ΗΟ ΓΑΙS ΚΑΛΟS

S.80.AE.291   Bareiss 46

148. Cup Type B, Fragmentary
Ca. 500 B.C.
Attributed to the Proto-Panaitian Group [Bothmer]
I: Jumper.
A: Horse race.
B: Hoplitodromos (foot race in armor).
Inscribed: ΛΕΑΛΡΟS [ΚΑΛΟS

S.82.AE.28

149. Cup Type B
Ca. 500-490 B.C.
I: Two youthful revelers.
A and B, each: satyr and a nude woman on either side of a column krater.

S.80.AE.325   Bareiss 84

*150. Cup Type B, Fragmentary
(See No. 36, pp. 50-53, figs. 36a-b.)
Ca. 500 B.C.
Attributed to Onesimos [Beazley]
I: Vomiting komast.
Inscribed: ΗΟ ΓΑΙS ΚΑΛΟS (retrograde)
A and B: Lovemaking.
More fragments of this cup are in the Louvre [D. Williams].

S.80.AE.305   Bareiss 327

*151. Cup Type B (See No. 36, pp. 50-53, fig. 36a-b.)
Ca. 490 B.C.
Attributed to Onesimos [Cahn]
Signed by Euphronios as potter [the complete signature recognized by Bothmer]: ΕΥΦΡ]ΟΝ[Ι]ΟS ΕΓΟΙΕ
I: Sick komast being attended by a friend.
A and B: Komos (komasts and women).

S.82.AE.35   Bareiss 229

*152. Cup Type B (See No. 30, pp. 44-45, figs. 30a-c.)
Ca. 490 B.C.
Attributed to the Brygos Painter [Bareiss]
I: Tekmessa running to cover the body of Aias.
A: Argument between Odysseus and Aias over the possession of the arms of Achilleus.
B: The casting of votes to award the arms.
Unmeaning inscriptions.
Etruscan graffito under the foot.

S.82.AE.27   Bareiss 346

One fragment is on loan from E. D. B. Vermeule [recognized by J. R. Guy]; another fragment is ex-Tübingen E36 [recognized by D. Williams].

153. Cup Type B
Ca. 480 B.C.
Attributed to the Brygos Painter [Cahn]
I: Youth in the palaestra with pick and javelins.
Inscribed: ΛΕΥΚΟΛΟΦΙΔΕS

S.80.AE.324   Bareiss 85

154. Cup Type B
Ca. 480 B.C.
Attributed to the Brygos Painter [Bothmer]
I: Youth with a lyre, holding a phorbeia (the mouth strap of a flute player) over a low altar.

S.82.AE.20   Bareiss 431

155. Cup Type B
Ca. 480 B.C.
Attributed to the Brygos Painter [Deppert]
I: Woman running to right with head turned back.

S.80.AE.321   Bareiss 53

*156. Cup Type B (See No. 34, pp. 48-50, fig. 34, color cover.)
Ca. 480 B.C.
Signed by Douris as painter: ΔΟRΙS [Ε]ΛΡΑΦSΕΝ
Potted by Python [Bothmer]
I: Schoolboy with a lyre facing a bearded man (his instructor?).
A and B: School scenes.
Inscribed, A: ΗΙΓΟΛΑΜΑ ΚΑΛΟS
B: ΗΙΓΟΛΑΜΑS [ΚΑ]ΛΟS

S.82.AE.36   Bareiss 47

157. Cup Type B (?)
Ca. 480 B.C.
Attributed to Makron [Beazley]
I: Satyr carrying a skyphos; between his feet, a shell.
The lower stem and foot are missing.

S.80.AE.251   Bareiss 359

*158. Cup Type B (See No. 33, p. 48, fig. 33.)
Ca. 480-470 B.C.
Attributed to Makron [Beazley]
I: Dancing reveler holding a kylix.
Inscribed: KALOS

S.82.AE.31   Bareiss 51

*159. Cup Type B (See No. 32, pp. 46-48, fig. 32.)
Ca. 480-470 B.C.
Attributed to the Briseis Painter [Beazley]
Signed by Brygos the potter on one handle: BRVΛOS EPOIESEN
I: Youth courting a girl who holds a mirror.
A and B: Men and youths dressed up as women (Anakreontists) dancing with attendants and musicians.

S.82.AE.37   Bareiss 241

160. Cup Type B
Ca. 470 B.C.
Attributed to the Foundry Painter [Beazley]
I: Lovemaking.
Inscribed: KA[L]OS LVK[O]S

S.80.AE.33   Bareiss 231

161. Cup Type B
Ca. 470 B.C.
Attributed to the Tarquinia Painter [Beazley]
I: Seated youth in himation, with a shield and a helmet shelf (or hook) hanging before him.
A and B: Symposion (A, three men, one playing the barbitos; B, man between two youths).
Unmeaning inscriptions.

S.80.AE.222   Bareiss 50

162. Cup Type B
Ca. 460 B.C.
Attributed to the Sabouroff Painter [Beazley]
I: Zeus. Inscribed in the exergue: ESATIK (interpreted as "to Attica")
A and B: Komos of old men, dressed up as women, dancing.
Etruscan graffito

S.80.AE.1

163. Cup Type B (?)
Ca. 430 B.C.
Attributed to the Eretria Painter [Bothmer]
I: Mounted warrior with spear and quiver, riding to left.
A: Three warriors, one of whom holds a horse.
B: Two warriors to right, one mounted and the other on foot beside his horse, looking back.

S.83.AE.15

*164. Cup Type B (See No. 29, p. 00, fig. 29.)
Ca. 420-410 B.C.
I: Nike flying toward a youth who holds a kithara and plectrum.
A and B: Two three-horse chariots with female charioteers racing to the left; the turning post for the race appears on Side A. The horses are branded, with an X on A, a kerykeion on B.

S.80.AE.290   Bareiss 358

*165. Cup Type C (See No. 28, p. 42, fig. 28.)
Ca. 510 B.C.
Attributed to the Ambrosios Painter [Beazley]
I: Young athlete pouring oil from an aryballos; against the wall behind him are javelins and a discus bag.
Inscribed: MNASIΛA

S.82.AE.19   Bareiss 230

166. Cup Type C Fragment
Ca. 510-500 B.C.
Attributed to Epiktetos [Bothmer]
I: Youth to right carrying a basket on his back.
Inscribed: EP[IK]TET[OS

S.80.AE.281

167. Cup Type C Fragment
Ca. 510-500 B.C.
Attributed to the Hermaios Painter [Beazley]
I: Figure of an oriental archer running to right with a tiny winged figure in a short chiton on his shoulders.
Inscribed: E]POIE

S.81.AE.1.1   Bareiss 72

168. Cup Type C
Ca. 500 B.C.
Attributed to Apollodoros [Bothmer]
I: Draped man standing before an altar; on the wall behind hang an aryballos, strigil, and sponge.
Inscribed: HO ΓΑΛΟS ΚΑΛΟS
(for HO ΓΑIS ΚΑΛΟS)

S.80.AE.248   Bareiss 357

169. Cup Type C Fragment (Lipped)
Ca. 470-460 B.C.
Attributed to the Painter of Agora P42 [Bothmer]
A: Two youths dressed in himatia to right; hanging on the wall, a lyre and a strigil.

S.81.AE.1.2

170. Cup Type C Fragment
Ca. 460 B.C.
Perhaps by a follower of Douris [Bothmer]
A: Bearded man to left, dressed in a himation; before him hang a sponge and aryballos; behind him, the beginnings of handle palmettes.
Inscribed: ΚΑ]ΛΕ

S.80.AE.54   Bareiss 405

171. Cup Fragment
Ca. 520-510 B.C.
Attributed to Oltos [Bothmer]
I: Maenad carrying a thyrsos (red leaves) and running to right looking back.
Inscribed: Η

S.80.AE.14   Bareiss 79

172. Cup Fragment
Ca. 510 B.C.
Attributed to the Euergides Painter [Bothmer]
I: Cock to right (feet remain).
Inscribed: E[Π]OI[ESEN]
A: Theseus and the Marathonian Bull.
B: Satyr carrying a wineskin; his name, Briachos, is inscribed: ΒΡΙΑ+ΟS
At the handles: Open palmettes.

S.80.AE.268   Bareiss 1D

173. Cup Fragments
Ca. 510-500 B.C.
Attributed to Epiktetos [Beazley]
A: Archer and warriors, one mounted(?); shield device: polypus
Inscribed: ΚΑΛΟS ; also inscribed:]EN

S.81.AE.1.3   Bareiss 403

174. Cup Fragment
Ca. 510-500 B.C.
Attributed to the Manner of the Epeleios Painter [Bothmer]
A: Head and shoulders of a youth wearing a wreath and brandishing a sword or club.

S.80.AE.191   Bareiss 257

175. Cup Fragment
Ca. 510-500 B.C.
Attributed to the Wider Circle of the Nikosthenes Painter [Bothmer]
I: Top of a wreathed head with a jumping weight behind it.
A: Four jumpers.

S.80.AE.44   Bareiss 265

176. Cup Fragment
Ca. 500 B.C.
Attributed to the Ambrosios Painter [Beazley]
A: Head of a fluting satyr to left.

S.80.AE.286   Bareiss 55

177. Cup Fragment
Ca. 500 B.C.
Near the Bonn Painter [Beazley]
I: Young warrior to right, holding a shield.

S.80.AE.186   Bareiss 61

178. Cup Fragment
Ca. 500-490 B.C.
Attributed to Onesimos [Bothmer]
Signed by Euphronios as potter [the complete signature recognized by Bothmer]
I: Bearded warrior to right, wearing a scalp on top of his helmet.
Inscribed: EVΦPONIJOS   EΠOIESEN
A: Battle of Lapiths and centaurs

S.80.AE.313   Bareiss 408

179. Cup Fragment
Ca. 500-490 B.C.
Attributed to Onesimos [Bothmer]
I: Head of youth with apicate fillet to left.
Inscribed: ΓΑΙS
A: Youth reaching with his left hand for a naked girl; another youth running up from the right.

S.80.AE.283   Bareiss 60

180. Cup Fragments
Ca. 490 B.C.
Attributed to Onesimos [Bothmer]
I: Youth taking a shower under a lionhead fountain, with another figure standing behind him; a pair of sandals hangs on the wall behind.
Inscribed: ΚΑ]ΛΟ[S (retrograde)

S.83.AE.5

181. Cup Fragments,
(White-ground, lipped inside)
(See No. 35, pp. 50-51, fig. 35.)
Ca. 490 B.C.
Attributed to Onesimos [Williams, Robertson]
Potted by Euphronios
I: Dionysos standing to right, holding a kantharos, attended by a satyr who stands before him to left, playing the double flutes.

S.82.AE.23

182. Cup Fragment
Ca. 490 B.C.
Attributed to Makron [Bothmer]
I: Courting scene (bearded man fondling a girl).
A: Two nereids running to the right.
More of the cup is in the Louvre [recognized by Bothmer].

S.80.AE.262   Bareiss 321

* **183. Cup Fragment** (See No. 31, p. 46, fig. 31.)
Ca. 480 B.C.
Attributed to the Brygos Painter [Cambitoglou]
A: Satyr with discus to right behind Dionysos or a maenad, also to right.

S.80.AE.277   Bareiss 54

184. Cup Fragment (Lipped inside)
Ca. 480-470 B.C.
Attributed to the Foundry Painter [Bothmer]
A: Youth in a himation to right, holding two staves, and the right hand of a hoplitodromos.
This fragment probably joins Louvre G290 [recognized by Bothmer].

S.80.AE.192   Bareiss 310

185. Cup Fragment
Ca. 470 B.C.
Attributed to the Tarquinia Painter [Bothmer]
I: Youth dipping his hands into the mouth of a large krater.
Inscribed:]ϟ ΚΑΛΟϟ

S.80.AE.282   Bareiss 417

186. Cup Fragment
Ca. 470-450 B.C.
Attributed to the Akestorides Painter [Beazley]
I: Seated boy reading from a scroll before his teacher.
Inscribed on the scroll:
    ΗΟΙΗΑ
    ΜΕΡΑΚ
    ΛΕΕΙ
    ΙΟΛΕΟ
(The text is from a forerunner of *Hyginus*).

S.80.AE.278   Bareiss 63

187. Cup Fragment
Ca. 460 B.C.
Attributed to the Painter of London D12 [Bothmer]
I: Warrior holding a shield to right.
A: Horse standing to right, next to a column.

S.80.AE.187   Bareiss 56

188. Cup Fragment
Ca. 460-450 B.C.
Attributed to the School of Makron [Bothmer]
A: Woman in chiton and himation standing to left with an apple in her right hand; before her, the hand of another figure holding a small fruit or flower.

S.80.AE.45   Bareiss 266

189. Cup Fragment
Ca. 460-450 B.C.
Attributed to the Aberdeen Painter [Bothmer]
I: Satyr pursuing a maenad.

S.80.AE.95   Bareiss 71

190. Cup Fragment
Ca. 460-450 B.C.
Attributed to a Follower of Makron, contemporary with the Telephos Painter [Beazley]
Two athletes with strigils in hand; on the wall behind, an alabastron suspended; on the left, a tendril from a floral.

S.82.AE.22   Bareiss 66

191. Stemless Cup Fragment
Ca. 460-450 B.C.
Attributed to a Follower of Douris [Beazley]
A: Woman to right, holding a barbitos, facing a man dressed in women's clothing; palmette beside the handle.

S.80.AE.13   Bareiss 67

192. Stemless Cup Fragment
Ca. 430 B.C.
I: Satyr seated to right on a low stool, holding a ball and fanning the flames of the low fire before him. Hanging behind, a wineskin. In the exergue, a one-handled drinking cup.
Inscribed: ΚΑ]ΛΟϟ

S.81.AE.1.4   Bareiss 267

193. Stemless Cup Fragment
Ca. 350 B.C.
I: Wreathed head of a youth to right.

S.81.AE.1.5

194. Lekanis Lid Fragment
Ca. 420-410 B.C.
Outside: figure of a woman (Amazon?) turned to left toward two spears of another figure.

S.80.AE.189   Bareiss 356

ATTIC BLACK WARE

195. Trefoil Oinochoe, Shape 2
Ca. 450 B.C.

S.80.AE.62   Bareiss 99

196. Skyphos of Corinthian shape
450-425 B.C.

S.80.AE.78   Bareiss 426

ETRUSCAN

197. Etrusco-Corinthian Olpe
First half of the sixth century B.C.
Attributed to the Bearded Sphinx Painter [Amyx]
Upper register: Confronted goats with swan behind the right one.
Lower register: Panthers on either side of a grazing goat; at the back, a swan.

S.80.AE.28   Bareiss 146

198. Etrusco-Corinthian Trefoil Oinochoe
First half of the sixth century B.C.
Attributed to the Volunteer Painter [Amyx]
Animal procession: Goat, boar, goat, swan, panther.
On the spout: Eyes.

S.80.AE.225

199. Bucchero Trefoil Oinochoe
First half of the sixth century B.C.
Incised animals (birds, panthers, leopard, goats, lion) and patterns.

S.82.AE.9   Bareiss 238

200. Bucchero Olpe
First half of the sixth century B.C.
Incised animals (birds, goat, lioness, boar, hound?) and patterns.

S.82.AE.10   Bareiss 246

201. Pontic (Etruscan) Neck Amphora Fragment
Ca. 575 B.C.
Attributed to the Paris Painter [Frel]
Judgment of Paris.
On the neck: Lotus and tendril.

S.80.AE.122   Bareiss 164

202. Pontic (Etruscan) Neck Amphora
Ca. 550 B.C.
Attributed to the Paris Painter [Bothmer]
On shoulders, in panels, A: Two mounted youths, carrying branches, with foxes running beside them;
B: The same, with a crane at the right end of the panel.
Below the panels, A: lion, panther, griffin, swan; B: griffin....siren.
The animal zone is divided by a hanging palmette under each handle. The lion has the same ears as the griffins.

S.80.AE.29   Bareiss 149

203. Black-figure Hydria Fragment
Ca. 500-490 B.C.
Attributed to the Micali Painter [Bothmer]
On the shoulder: A palmette.
On the body: A dancer.

S.82.AE.13   Bareiss 165

204. Skyphos Fragment
Ca. 350 B.C.
May be attributed to the Sokra Group [Bothmer]
Ithyphallic satyr to right added in superposed colors.

S.80.AE.125   Bareiss 169

SICILIAN

***205. Squat Lekythos Fragment**
(See No. 45, p. 62, fig. 45.)
Ca. 350-325 B.C.
Attributed to the Lentini Group [Bothmer]
Fluting satyr reclining on a wineskin.

S.80.AE.243   Bareiss 163

206. Pyxis with Lid
Ca. 330 B.C.
Grape vines.

S.80.AE.57a and b   Bareiss 427

APULIAN VASES

207. Pelike, Fragmentary
Ca. 350 B.C.
A: Dionysos and Ariadne with two satyrs, one fluting and one dancing, two Erotes, and one seated maenad.

S.80.AE.289   Bareiss 211

208. Pelike Fragment
Ca. 375 B.C.
Attributed to the Circle of the Black Fury Group
A: Woman to left seated on throne.

S.80.AE.309   Bareiss 181

209. Volute Krater Fragment
Ca. 350 B.C.
Attributed to the Circle of the Darius Painter
A: Seated Zeus dressed in a himation.

S.80.AE.130   Bareiss 175

210. Volute(?) Krater Fragment
Ca. 350 B.C.
A: Woman to right carrying an amphora; behind her, a herm; in front of her, a winged figure.

S.80.AE.172   Bareiss 399

211. Volute Krater Fragment (Neck)
Ca. 350 B.C.
A: Three horses from a wheeling chariot.

S.80.AE.133   Bareiss 183

212. Volute Krater Fragment (Neck)
Ca. 350 B.C.
Attributed to the Varrese Painter [Bothmer]
A: Three-quarter facing female head in center of elaborate floral decoration.

S.80.AE.316   Bareiss 187

213. Volute Krater Fragments (Two, from the body)
Ca. 350 B.C.
1: Palmettes, Hermes, figure of a pedagogue.
2: Seated satyr who holds a syrinx and a club.

S.80.AE.131.1 and 2   Bareiss 176a and b

214. Calyx Krater Fragment
Ca. 375 B.C.
A: Dionysos reclining to left in a naiskos, holding a kantharos.

S.80.AE.195   Bareiss 198

215. Calyx Krater Fragment
Ca. 375 B.C.
A: Gigantomachy: Two warriors in a duel, with a thunderbolt between them and hands, perhaps of a fallen figure, from the upper level of the scene.

S.80.AE.138   Bareiss 194

216. Calyx Krater Fragment
Ca. 350 B.C.
Two phlyakes (comic actors) at an altar.

S.82.AE.52   Bareiss 404

217. Calyx Krater Fragment
Ca. 350 B.C.
Attributed to the Underworld Painter
In two levels, upper: Seated figure, shield, seated woman; lower: Zeus, youth (Apollo?), Hermes, bull's head.

S.80.AE.143   Bareiss 204

218. Calyx Krater Fragment
Ca. 350 B.C.
Attributed to the Darius Painter [Oliver]
A: Herakles, with bow and club, threatening Busiris.
B: Chariot race with turning post.

S.80.AE.263   Bareiss 192a and b

219. Calyx Krater Fragment
Ca. 350 B.C.
A: Old man to left, looking at a winged animal (Pegasos?) or figure before him; behind him, a tripod.

S.80.AE.141   Bareiss 199

220. Calyx Krater Fragment
Ca. 325 B.C.
A: Achilleus killing Penthesilea; a tree and the arm of another figure on the right.

S.80.AE.287   Bareiss 179

*221. Bell Krater Fragment
(See No. 44, pp. 60-61, fig. 44.)
Ca. 390-380 B.C.
Attributed to the Black Fury Group [Trendall]
Scylla carrying a trident and a shell, facing a sea-bull (carrying Europa?).

S.82.AE.8   Bareiss 205

222. Bell Krater Fragment
Ca. 375 B.C.
Attributed to the Hoppin Painter [Trendall]
One woman holding a basket on her left knee and a second dancing before Dionysos, who reclines on the right.

S.80.AE.236   Bareiss 191

*223. Bell Krater Fragment
(See No. 43, p. 60, fig. 43.)
Ca. 375 B.C.
A: Cassandra (?, hair only) crouching before a comic statue of Athena.

S.80.AE.242   Bareiss 185

224. Bell Krater Fragment
Ca. 350 B.C.
A: Satyr holding a syrinx, looking round to left at a seated maenad(?).

S.80.AE.135   Bareiss 189

225. Bell Krater Fragment
Ca. 350 B.C.
A: Orestes at the Delphic Omphalos; Apollo stands on the left, holding a laurel staff; the Delphic tripod stands behind Orestes and the Omphalos.
S.80.AE.264   Bareiss 184

226. Bell Krater Fragment
Ca. 350 B.C.
Attributed to the Lykurgus Painter [Bothmer]
A: Man to right, looking back, carrying a large lidded object decorated with a frieze of silhouetted figures below triglyphs.
S.80.AE.137   Bareiss 193

227. Bell Krater Fragment
Ca. 350 B.C.
A: Youth to right, looking back.
S.80.AE.55   Bareiss 410

228. Krater Fragment
Ca. 375 B.C.
A: Suppliant king (Priam?) facing left and the arm of a woman who stands beside him.
S.80.AE.314   Bareiss 180

229. Krater Fragment
Ca. 350 B.C.
A: Head of a bridled horse to left.
S.80.AE.132   Bareiss 177

230. Krater Fragment (Calyx or Bell)
Ca. 350 B.C.
Attributed to the Lykurgus Painter
A: Old satyr fluting before a seated maenad.
S.80.AE.140   Bareiss 196

231. Krater Fragment
Ca. 350 B.C.
Attributed to the Darius Painter [Oliver]
A: Head of a woman to right, next to a winged figure; behind her, a bull's head and a phiale.
S.80.AE.144   Bareiss 206

232. Pelike Fragment
Ca. 350 B.C.
A: Youth offering a kithara to a seated woman who holds two flutes; there are two feet about the head of the youth (Eros?).
S.80.AE.145   Bareiss 207

233. Hydria or Pelike Fragment
Ca. 400 B.C.
Connected with the Black Fury Painter [Oliver]
A: Youth with a horse (Dioskouros?) beside a woman (Medea?) holding a phiale; another figure on the right.
S.80.AE.312   Bareiss 171

234. Hydria or Pelike Fragment
Ca. 375 B.C.
Head of an old man to right; above, the fingers of a right hand.
S.80.AE.128   Bareiss 173

235. Squat Lekythos, Fragmentary
Ca. 370 B.C.
Attributed to the Hoppin Painter [Trendall]
Five or more girls holding hands in a dance around an altar.
S.80.AE.30   Bareiss 166

236. Footed Alabastron
Ca. 350 B.C.
Attributed to the Alabastra Group [Trendall]
A: Running woman holding a fan and wreath.
B: Bust of a woman in the center of an elaborate floral motif.
S.80.AE.330

237. Skyphos Fragment
Ca. 375 B.C.
Attributed to the Group of Naples 3231 [Oliver]
A: Lovers on a couch with attendants standing on either side and an observer looking through the window above them.
S.80.AE.267   Bareiss 409

238. Skyphos Fragment
Ca. 375 B.C.
Head, shoulders, and right hand of a phlyax (comic actor).
S.80.AE.239   Bareiss 178

239. Skyphos Fragment
Ca. 330 B.C.
Head of a bearded man to left.
S.80.AE.108   Bareiss 128

240. Skyphos
Ca. 330 B.C.
A and B: Head of a woman in a sakkos.
S.80.AE.56   Bareiss 421

GNATHIAN

241. Calyx Krater Fragment
Ca. 350 B.C.
B: Satyr to left, holding a torch before him (incised, with added white for hair and torch).

S.80.AE.311   Bareiss 197

242. Bell Krater Fragment
Ca. 325 B.C.
A: Eros flying to right with tympanum before Leda and the Swan.

S.80.AE.159   Bareiss 353

243. Squat Lekythos
Ca. 330 B.C.
Eros holding a mirror and garland.

S.80.AE.71   Bareiss 304

*244. Oinochoe, Shape 10 (See No. 46, p. 00, fig. 46.)
Ca. 350 B.C.
Boy wrestling with Pan.
Plastic female heads on the sides of the handle.

S.80.AE.331

245. Stemless Cup
Late fourth century B.C.
I: Four stamped palmettes in the center; ivy fruits and leaves on incised stems around inner lip.

S.80.AE.75   Bareiss 420

246. Stemless Cup
Late fourth century B.C.
I: Three stamped palmettes in the center; ivy fruits and leaves on incised stems around inner lip.

S.80.AE.74   Bareiss 419

CAMPANIAN

247. Black-figure Neck Amphora
Ca. 500 B.C.
On the neck, A: Tiny owl between spirals and palmettes; B: Two running Gorgons.

S.80.AE.240

248. Fish Plate
Ca. 320 B.C.
Torpedo fish and two perch.

S.80.AE.67   Bareiss 200

LUCANIAN

249. Amphora Fragment, Panathenaic Shape
Ca. 400 B.C.
Attributed to the Amykos Painter [Oliver]
Originally in two registers; beneath a cyma pattern, youth pursuing a girl (Peleus and Thetis?) while another girl runs away to the left.

S.80.AE.327   Bareiss 42

250. Bell Krater Fragment
Ca. 400 B.C.
Attributed to the Amykos Painter [Bothmer]
Head and shoulders of a woman to left.

S.80.AE.261   Bareiss 412

251. Bell Krater Fragment
Ca. 400 B.C.
Attributed to the Dolon Painter [Trendall]
Departure of warriors (two armed youths with a woman and bearded man).

S.80.AE.259   Bareiss 148

252. Calyx Krater Fragment
Ca. 350 B.C.
Attributed to the Creusa Painter [Oliver]
A: Woman seated to left, looking back.

S.80.AE.109   Bareiss 131

ARRETINE

*253. Bowl (See No. 47, p. 65, fig. 47.)
Later first century B.C.
Stamped with name PERENNI
Around the outside: Symplegmata. The unglazed bowl was perhaps broken before glazing and fired as test pieces [Bothmer].

S.82.AE.14.1 and 2   Bareiss 411

LEAD-GLAZE

254. Skyphos
Second century B.C.
From Asia Minor
Green outside, yellow within, imitating metal.
Garlands of pinecones.
Beneath handles: Masks of Silenus suspended.

S.80.AE.72   Bareiss 343

255. Skyphos
Hellenistic
Green outside, golden yellow within, imitating metal.
Seated figure contemplating statue of Priapos, standing figure with a lance, walking figure, flying Nike.

S.80.AE.81

256. Jar
Hellenistic
Brown
All-over pattern of raised points.

S.80.AE.76   Bareiss 423

257. Bottle
Hellenistic
Green
Scale pattern (or feathers).

S.80.AE.77   Bareiss 424

BRONZE

Etruscan Mirror
Ca. 350-325 B.C.
Attributed to the Z Group
Achilleus and Chryseis seated in the company of Aphrodite and another female attendant (names inscribed). The handle is decorated with floral patterns and a mule's head terminal.

S.82.AC.11   Bareiss 349

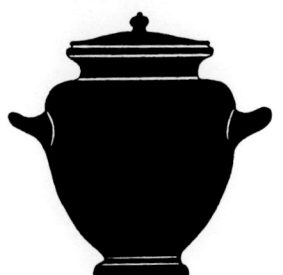
Stamnos

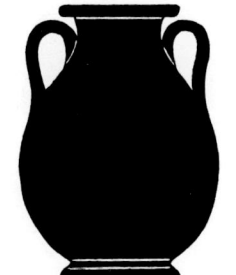
Pelike

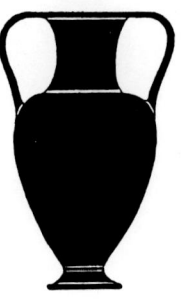
Nicosthenic Amphora

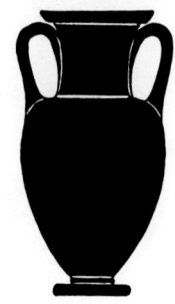
Neck Amphora

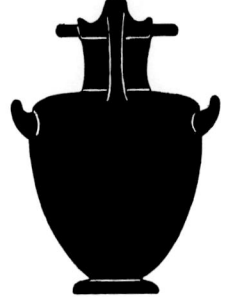
Hydria

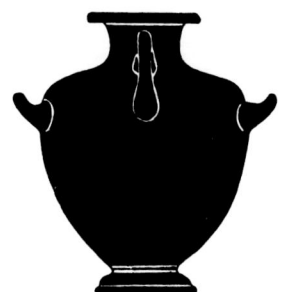
Kalpis

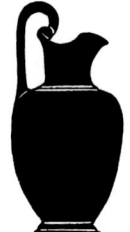
Trefoil Oinochoe

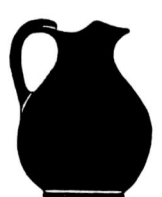
Oinochoe Shape 3 (Chous)

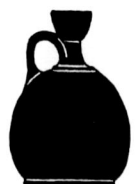
Squat Lekythos

Epinetron

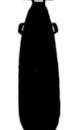
Alabastron

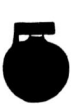
Aryballos

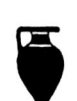
Proto-Corinthian Pointed Aryballos

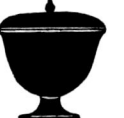
Nicosthenic Pyxis

Tripod Pyxis

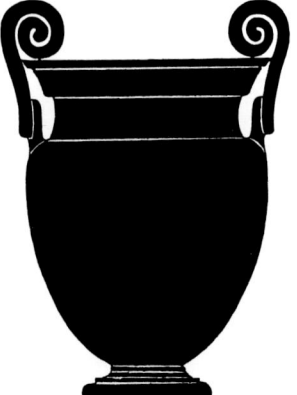
Volute Krater

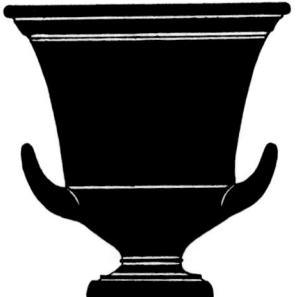
Calyx Krater

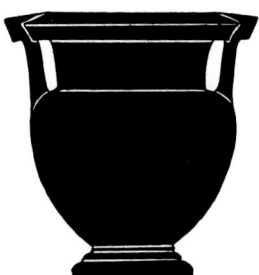
Column Krater

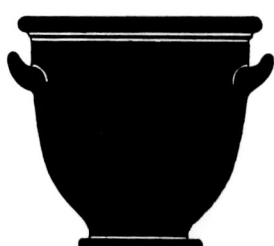
Bell Krater

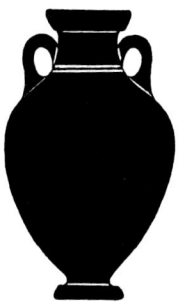 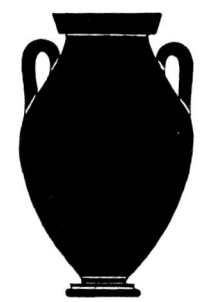 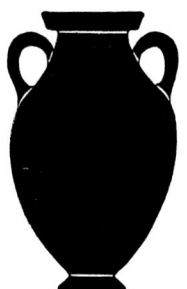 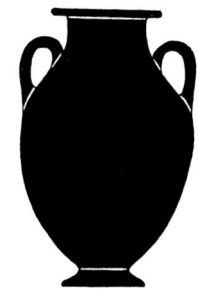

| Panathenaic Amphora | Amphora Type A | Amphora Type B | Amphora Type C |

 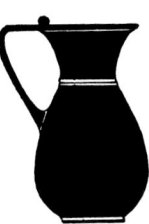 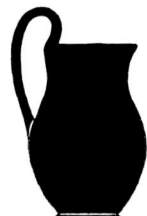 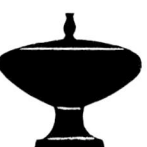 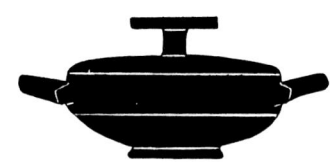

| Lekythos | Non-Attic Olpe | Attic Olpe | Exaleiptron | Lekanis |

 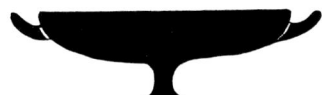 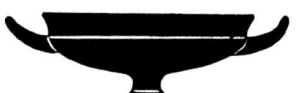

| Cup Type A | Cup Type B | Cup Type C |

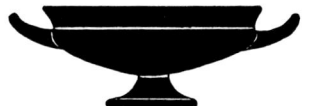  

| Siana Cup | Lip Cup | Stemless Cup |

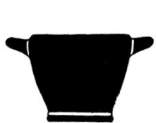 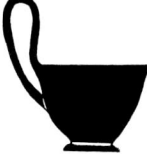 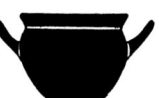

| Skyphos | Kyathos | Mastoid Cup |